# The Art of Macramé
## Modern Design in Knotting

Joan Fisher

**HAMLYN**
London · New York · Sydney · Toronto

Shown in photograph on front cover: blue
macramé shawl, knotted in heavy cord,
by Bo Ridley.

Shown in photographs on back cover:
'Fiesta' wall hanging in knitting wool and
wooden beads, by Pauline Oddy, 2nd year
home economics student at Bath College of
Education; sculptured head mask in parcel
string, by Marion Hicks, 2nd year diploma
student in art and design at Goldsmiths'
College, London; green suede handbag with
macramé insert worked in synthetic tubular
cord, by Mrs. Joan Fogg, of Bromley, Kent.

Published by
The Hamlyn Publishing Group Ltd
London - New York - Sydney - Toronto
Hamlyn House, Feltham, Middlesex, England

Printed by Litografía A. Romero, S. A.,
Santa Cruz de Tenerife, Canary Islands, Spain

# Contents

# Introduction

I do not claim to be a macramé expert. I discovered macramé only recently – almost by accident – but became immediately enthralled by its simplicity, effectiveness and versatility.

As I am still virtually a novice to the craft no part of the technique of knotting is 'second nature' to me, and my mind is full of the sort of questions that will no doubt occur to you if you too are coming fresh to the craft. Questions such as: how do I finish off work, what do I do with loose ends, how can I join one piece of knotting to another, how can I 'shape' a curved edge...? The answers to all these – and many more – problems can be found in this book, as well as full and detailed instructions for knotting techniques, and suggestions for both traditional and modern applications of knotting patterns.

One of the many joys of macramé is its universal appeal. Knitting and crochet are usually considered to be the prerogatives of women. Macramé is very much for all – for men, women and children, for young and old. It is supremely creative, satisfying and soothing, and its therapeutic qualities such that the craft is now being used widely in hospitals for occupational therapy.

Children especially find a strong appeal in the simplicity of the technique, where no needles, hooks or other tools are required. My twelve-year-old stepdaughter, Caroline, who has never shown any great aptitude for needlework or handicrafts before has become a macramé enthusiast, and is fast designing and making belts, bags and other items for herself and her school friends. The three-colour belt on page 144 and bag on page 154 are her designs, made after only about ten minutes' tuition in the two basic knots.

The scope of macramé, unlike most other crafts, goes far beyond the published pattern. Even if you have never designed so much as a straight line before, once you have acquired a working knowledge of knotting procedures, your mind will probably be teeming with new ideas for projects and patterns.

This is why I have touched only lightly upon sculptural three-dimensional knotting. I take you through the fascinating history of the subject, the myriad details of knotting techniques, and offer a few patterns for practical and decorative items to make. Sculptural design is the step beyond, where you yourself take over.

There is nothing magical or particularly difficult about sculptural work: it is no more complex than working in the round, which is fully explained in the chapter starting on page 96. But such work is the most personal form of modern macramé design, and if you reach this stage then there is nothing further I can tell you or teach you about this delightful and exciting art.

Inevitably you will adapt macramé to suit your own requirements, and your own tastes: for instance, you may wish only to make braids for trimming purposes, or fashion outfits and accessories from coloured knitting wools, or maybe you will work exclusively in traditional style with fine yarns and lacy patterns. Whichever way you choose to interpret the age-old craft of macramé, I can guarantee you will enjoy many happy hours of creative satisfaction.

Two final points: the names of knots and knotting techniques vary considerably from one reference source to another. At the first mention of each term, I specify which name will be used throughout the book, but I also list some of the other versions which exist, and which you may come across elsewhere.

Secondly, the words thread, end, cord and yarn are virtually interchangeable, but in an attempt to clarify the particular usage of each term in this book, specific meanings should be taken as follows: thread usually refers to the cut lengths of yarn before being set on; after the threads have been doubled and set on to a holding cord the resulting working lengths are termed ends; working ends are referred to as cords in pattern instructions; and yarn is a general term covering all working materials, natural and synthetic, from string and plastic through to wool and nylon.

JOAN FISHER

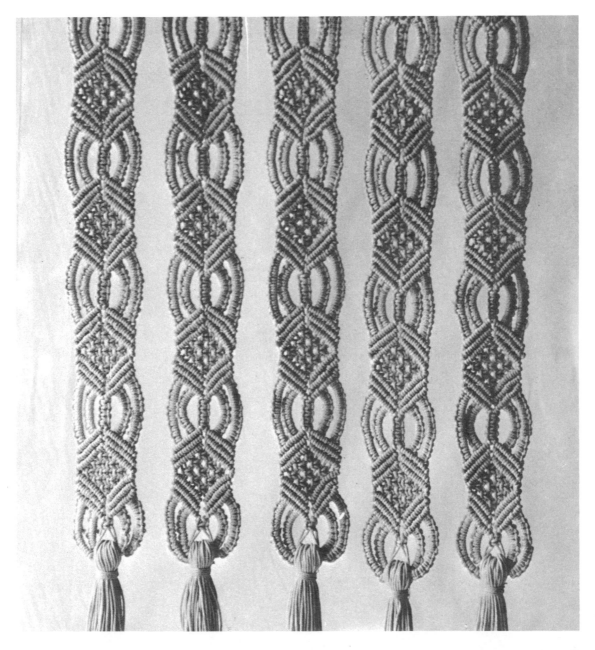

# How it all began

The knot is as old as time. Long before the invention of glue or sticky tape, nails or safety pins, the only way to keep things together or to suspend them or to pull them along, was to tie a knot. The knot could be tied in the object itself, if it was sufficiently pliable, or by binding with plant fibres, strips of animal skins, human hair, long grasses or stems.

The knotted form therefore goes back to the dawn of history, and the tying of a knot is an act almost as instinctive to the human race as breathing, sleeping, eating or drinking. Gorillas are reputed today to tie knots in creepers to keep their nests together.

From a purely functional beginning it was not long before the decorative value of the knotted form was appreciated and exploited. And throughout history while knots continued to play an important practical part in the everyday lives of almost every race and community, alongside this were developed many types of ornamental and fancy knotting. The Chinese people are believed to have been the first to use knots in their ornamental form, and since ancient times the Japanese have used a series of knots for ceremonial purposes.

Just think how even today knots punctuate our lives from the moment we are born: in babyhood dainty ribbon knots decorate bonnets, bootees, jackets and dresses; functionally they serve to keep bibs and napkins in place. As we grow up, we tie up parcels with string, thread ribbons in our hair, knot ties around our necks, belts around our waists, and laces in our shoes.

Every profession, trade and calling has evolved its own series of knots: surgeons knot incisions together, gardeners knot twine round plants. Housewives have their own series of everyday knots, so do fishermen, builders, butchers, mountaineers, and — above all — sailors.

The macramé knot could be called the needlewoman's knot, and yet this is a misnomer because no needle is required for its execution. Also, because of its nautical associations, it could be — and in fact often is — claimed as the sailor's knot. It can be described as a regularised form of decorative knotting, and has its foundation in the knots that go back to the beginning of time.

Knots similar to those used in macramé work can be seen in the remains of many ancient civilisations. Examples of elaborate knotting in flax, rawhide and papyrus, have been found in Egyptian tombs, some known to date from over 3,500 years ago. Mummy wrappings have been found ornamented with drawn work, cut work and other open ornamentation that implies a knotting technique. Galley sails for primitive sailing boats were rich in knotted rigging.

The traditional lozenge pattern found in most forms of lace and in macramé work can be seen on the coats of ancient Danes, where borders are edged with a network of this pattern. A remnant of a piece of gold lace, blackened and decayed, but still clearly showing the lozenge motif, was dug up from a Scandinavian barrow at Wareham, in England, in the 18th century.

## The early use of plaiting

One of the earliest craft forms we learn as a child is to plait three strands of fibre together to form a decorative braid. This is a simple technique yet infinitely satisfying. Little wonder therefore that plaiting appears on very many examples of early craftsmanship: decorated skulls and ritual masks from tribal Africa, India, New Guinea, North America, Fiji Islands—to name but a few—show plaiting, sometimes threaded with beads.

A headhunter's trophy from Assam shows an enemy head decorated with buffalo horns and knotted tassels of grass. Peruvian mummies often had their hair arranged in demure plaits. Footballs from Borneo were made of plaited rattan; sandals from Bengal were made from plaited flax; and models of sacred huts were made from plaited coconut fibre.

Long before the simplest weaving was discovered, fabrics for clothing, for decoration, for play and for work could be fashioned only from plaiting and knotting

Maori chiefs wore cloaks with kiwi feathers and coloured wool plaiting. Jewellery from the Solomon Islands included wristlets of beads worked in with plaited vegetable fibres. In the Horniman Museum, London, a highly decorated pendant from the Solomon Islands can be seen, made from shells, coloured beads, rodents' teeth, nut shells and pierced bone attached to a thick plaited fibre rope.

Soon primitive people began to plait and twist plant and animal fibres into immensely strong ropes. Bridges were suspended from such ropes, fishing nets were made from it, huts supported by it, ships rigged with it.

Both savage tribes and civilised communities alike developed ropemaking and knotting at similar levels, although the materials used were usually different—the Indian tribes of Vancouver Island, for instance, are known to have twisted sinews of whales into three-strand rope, merely because the whale sinews happened to be close at hand.

## Writing in knots

Apart from their decorative and practica functions, knots played another very important part in history. In the ancient Inca civilisation of Peru, the art of writing was never discovered; instead an elaborate system of recording and sending messages was

*Ancient Peruvian quipu – knots were tied in cords to convey messages and record history.*

devised, based on a series of knotted cords.

A number of vertical cords were suspended from a horizontal cord about 2 ft. long — almost exactly similar to the setting-on arrangement of threads for macramé work today — knots were tied in the cords, and according to the type of knot, its position on the cord, its relation to the other knots, and the colour of the cord, a message was conveyed.

This knotted message 'chart' was called a *quipu*, coming from the Peruvian word meaning 'knot'. The nearer the knot was to the horizontal cord, the more important the subject to which it referred. A white cord usually symbolised peace or purity, a yellow one meant gold, a red one war or danger, a green one grain, and a black one death.

Births, marriages and deaths were recorded by this method, and other important statistics of the Inca civilisation. Military chiefs frequently received their orders by despatches of *quipus*.

As well as using knotted strings to record history and events, a similar device was used for a decimal system of numbers. The

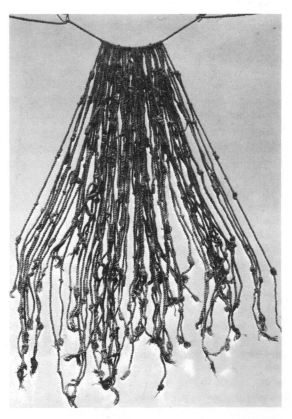

colours of the cords were not significant here, but the knots and their positions were. A single overhand knot at the bottom of a cord represented the figure 1, a double overhand knot was 2, and so on up to 9. These units were all positioned at the lower ends of the cords. The tens, following a similar knotting sequence, were positioned above the units, and then the hundreds above the tens, and the thousands above the hundreds. As well as recording large sums, this early form of accounts ledger also noted dates and astronomical data.

Even today Peruvian shepherds are believed still to keep a tally on their flocks of sheep by means of knotted cords.

Similarly in ancient China, before an alphabet was invented, the Chinese used knots both to record history and to act as memory aids. The tying of a knot in a pocket handkerchief as a device to jog our memory is based on the primitive Chinese system. Similar knotted string memory aids were used in many countries, and in many civilisations, including Tibet, Mexico and Persia. From this early 'knot writing' evolved the tally stick, where notches were cut in wood or stone to convey messages.

The North American Indian tribes also used knotted cords to record dates, but they took the system a step further with their wampum belts. These ingenious belts were made from coloured shell beads strung close together on cords, or sometimes the beads were embroidered on to deerskin. The particular arrangements of the beads, their colours, and their size all had significance. The belts were worn as ornaments, and according to the patterning it was possible to tell at a glance the wearer's place in society, his achievements, and his family history.

The colour significance was similar to that of the *quipu* – white for peace, red for war, black for death. These colours have the same symbolic meanings to us today: red denotes danger, and is used on traffic lights, and on warning notices; similarly black is the colour of mourning or death, and white worn by brides as a symbol of purity. If an Indian chief was defeated in battle, he would surrender his wampum belt to his victor. The wampum shell beads were also used as money but were then usually only

coloured purple and white.

Elaborate patterns could be depicted on the wampum belts, and a style of macramé work which is similar in appearance is called wampum weaving. This in fact was the forerunner of a technique later perfected in Italy and called Cavandoli work (see page 92). Both techniques are based upon closely worked knotting and the use of a contrast colour to create a shape or figure on a background colour.

### First knotted fringes

One of the very earliest uses of decorative knotting in clothing can be seen in the heavily fringed cloaks and tunics depicted in Byzantine mosaics and Assyrian sculptures. An Assyrian frieze, dated c. 850 BC, in the British Museum, London, shows a military chief with a deep knotted fringe along the bottom edge of his tunic and also on the harness of his horse.

It is easy to see why such fringing came about: when cloth is woven loose warp ends of thread remain at either end. To trim these ends away leaves a hard abrupt edge, so in any age when embellishment to costume was considered desirable – and there are few eras in history where this has not been the case – these warp ends were left to form a fringe. To knot the ends of the fringe into a decorative pattern was a natural development.

In a similar way, the Iroquois Indians who wore shirts and dresses made from native buckskin soon found after fashioning a garment if the excess buckskin was trimmed away the small pieces were not much use for anything else and had to be discarded. Far better – and more ornamental – to leave the excess skin on the garment but slit it to form fringes.

From this early beginning evolved the traditional American Indian clothes with their heavy fringing and elaborate trimmings, a style which in recent years has become fashionable in countries throughout the world. Macramé knotting lends itself admirably to all forms of the Indian dress 'cult', both in the garments themselves, in jewellery, and in accessories.

### The knot in art

Throughout history the knot is represented in most art forms, both in its natural state and as a design motif. In the paintings and drawings of the early Greeks, Romans and Egyptians, however, an interesting anomaly exists: although the pictures show an almost photographic and minutely detailed reproduction of contemporary events, situations and people, whenever a knot was indicated it was shown merely by a coil of rope or cord looped in position. The knot itself was clearly not tied. In fact in all the art of this period, a completely tied knot is significantly absent.

The reason for this is not known, but one theory suggests an old superstition which believed that if an artist drew a knot which could not be untied, either he, or the subject of the painting, would become the victim of a dreadful fate.

The reef knot — popularly called Hercules knot because it was believed to have been invented by the famous Greek hero — was attributed with magical powers. Pliny wrote that wounds would heal more rapidly if the bandages which bound them were tied with Hercules knots.

The form of the reef knot appears frequently in classical architecture, and also in the jewellery of the Hellenistic period (3rd century BC) where it is known as the Heracles, or Heraclian, knot. The motif frequently formed the centres of magnificent diadems, often inlaid with garnets and hung with pendants, and was believed to hasten the healing of wounds.

In primitive art, right up until the Christian era, the imitation of the works of God was forbidden to many races and even vegetation was not permitted as a motif for ornamentation. It was natural therefore that geometric patterns were devised, many based on the beauty of the knotted form. The Chinese used small interknotted symbols in their early art, and the Pictish School of Celtic Art used knotwork extensively: the circular knotwork motif can be seen in the St. Andrew's Cross of Scotland.

Knots also were used on heraldic devices. The Carrick bend (or Josephine knot, as it is more usually known today) was used as an heraldic badge by Hereward Wake.

From more recent years, there are a number of paintings in which macramé knotting can be seen: *The Repast of Simon the Pharisee*, by the 16th century painter Paul Veronese shows a cloth with a macramé fringe; while *Last Supper*, by Sebastian Ricci has a tablecloth which appears to be edged with a macramé border. There are also paintings by lesser known artists in the Cathedrals of Spain where macramé work is indicated.

The most famous legendary knot undoubtedly is the Gordian knot. Zeus proclaimed that whoever untied this knot would reign over Asia, but all attempts to unravel the intricate knot failed dismally until Alexander the Great came along and took the easy way out. He simply slashed through the knot with his sword. It seems rather like cheating but nevertheless he later ruled over Asia, just as the prediction had foretold. No one knows why the knot was so impossible to untie but a likely explanation is that the ends had been cleverly concealed inside the centre of the knot.

## Magic and the supernatural

Knots have also long been associated with magic, the occult and superstition, having both malign and benign characteristics. Arabian witches worked spells by blowing on knots, and in the 16th century it was believed in many northern countries that witches could tie up the wind in knots.

Sailors bought these so-called strings of knotted winds from the witches, and when becalmed at sea would untie a knot in the hope that a favourable wind would at once be forthcoming. The knots were in groups of three: the first knot in the string was reputed to bring a moderate wind, the second knot a more dramatic gale, and the third a near-hurricane.

In many primitive races, superstitions concerning pregnant women were associated with knots. Such women, and often their husbands as well, were forbidden to wear any form of knot or knotted garment — or even to sit cross-legged — until safely delivered of the child. This superstition is probably the basis for the belief in Scandinavian countries that the knot symbol could act as a form of birth control. In order to curtail their families, the last-born son was named Canute (meaning knot), the idea being that this would prevent a further conception. There is no evidence to show whether this method was effective!

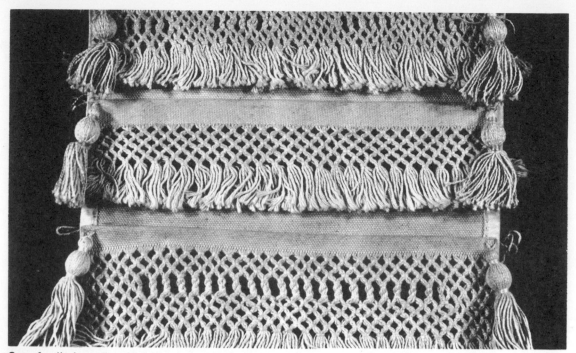

*Set of sailor's wall pockets in canvas with macramé panels, each divided into pockets.*

The cat's cradle, played with string by children, has since early times been associated with the symbols of birth, life and growth.

In ancient Egypt, where magic was closely linked with healing, knots had an important part to play. They were believed both to be able to cause and to cure illness. Magicians cast spells to heal the sick, and the spells invariably were accompanied by the tying of magical knots. Certain knots such as a sevenfold one were considered more efficacious than others!

In some European countries, it was believed if a fever-ridden person tied knots in the limbs of a willow tree — one knot for every day of the fever — then muttered a few well-chosen magic words, the tree would acquire the fever, and the patient would be cured. Knots were also used to eliminate warts — knots were tied in a string, one knot for each wart, then the string was buried under a stone. By the time the string had rotted, it was believed the wart-sufferer would be cured.

## The sailors' contribution

Although knotwork developed at similar levels in most civilisations and most parts of the world, much of the spread of particular knot forms must be attributed to the early mariners.

Volumes could be devoted to the knots and knotwork of the mariners of yesterday and today, for it is a craft which still continues to maintain interest in nautical circles, and has a fascinating language of its own: a language which abounds in splices and bends, seizings and stopperings, shippings and shortenings; where knots are never tied but are put in, made fast or cast, where tangles are cleared, jammed knots are opened, and hitches are taken.

The seafaring man is the supreme master of knot-tying: it is a joy to watch him as he secures a vast seagoing vessel to a quayside with a beautifully neat and deceptively simple turn of the rope.

Ever since man first took to the sea, long voyages have meant endless hours to while away and when the sailor was 'off duty' he needed something to occupy his mind and hands. Diversions in the early days of sailing were few, so the sailor had to find his own amusement. Various crafts were developed including knitting, basketwork and carving, but the majority of seafarers turned to knotting.

Knots after all were a natural way of life to them, there was a plentiful supply of materials by way of ropes, twine and fishing line on board ship, and knotting was easy to do even in cramped quarters. So the sailors began experimenting with ornamental knotting, and to make all manner of trimmings for their ship's 'furniture' — bells were adorned with knotted pulls; capstan wheels were covered with elaborately patterned knotted fabrics; wall pockets were made to hang by the sailor's bunk and hold his possessions; fringes were knotted for sea chest covers. Even eye screens for accommodation ladders were made to protect the modesty of lady passengers when they ascended or descended to their cabins!

Knot boards showing samples of the sailors' fancy knotwork were prepared, similar to the embroidery samplers of Victorian ladies. Many of these knot boards can be seen in maritime museums throughout the world and often in the homes of seafaring men.

It was not long before the sailor realised he could put his handicraft to profitable use and he began to knot items to barter in foreign lands: knotted belts, bottle covers, handbags, and many other decorative items for personal and household adornment were made and traded whenever the ship came into port. And so knots as a craft form spread to countries throughout the world.

With the advent of radio, reading matter, and other such portable 'diversions', knotting as a chief pastime of sailors sadly faded from the scene. But seafaring men today still enthusiastically talk about their knots and contribution to the field of fancy knotting with a certain proprietary air!

## The birth of macramé lace

Around the 14th century a craft similar to the macramé knotting we know today was being done in France, although it was not at this time known as macramé. After a brief spell of popularity however, general interest in the craft faded.

The nuns, superb exponents of all forms of needlework, were quick to see the possibilities of decorative knotting, and the craft was adopted in the convents. Along with other fine needlework, crochet and knitting, knotted bordering of ecclesiastical linen was worked in heavy, stiff yarns.

At this time all forms of needlework were held in great esteem and women particularly skilled with their needle were honoured and respected. This applied above all to the nuns, and the highest accolade one could pay to a young girl was to suggest her needlework was so perfect it was 'as if she had been brought up in a convent'.

The importance of being an accomplished needlewoman was apparently maintained for some centuries and widespread throughout Europe. In 1614 the King of Siam applied to James I of Britain for an English wife. A suitable young lady was offered, described by her father as being of excellent parts for 'music, her needle and good discourse'. An epitaph to one Catherine Sloper who died in 1620, and is buried in the cloisters of Westminster Abbey, declares she was 'exquisite at her needle'.

Macramé in the form of heavy fringes, braids and medallions had been an established art in Arabia since the 13th century. The Spaniards learned the technique from the Moors, and the returning Crusaders introduced the art to Italy. Here, and particularly at Genoa, was born macramé lace, a far finer, more delicate form of the work than the heavy knotting previously done by the Arabs, and — in a different way — by the French nuns.

The Italians who claim the invention of point (*punto*) or needlemade lace evolved macramé along with the many other beautiful laces of the Renaissance period. The work was known as *punto a gropo*, or *gropari. Groppo* or *gruppo* means a knot or tie, hence the term meant knotted lace.

The work was first carried out on the unwoven ends of a fabric as it left the loom and as the threads for the fabric were fine, so too was the knotted fringe. Soon borders and inserts were being made separately in cream silks and unbleached threads and then either combined with other laces or used to trim garments and household linen.

The examples illustrated on page 12 show how exquisitely fine was the knotting of this period and how difficult it is to tell the difference between it and the needlemade and bobbin laces. *Punto a gropo* had no

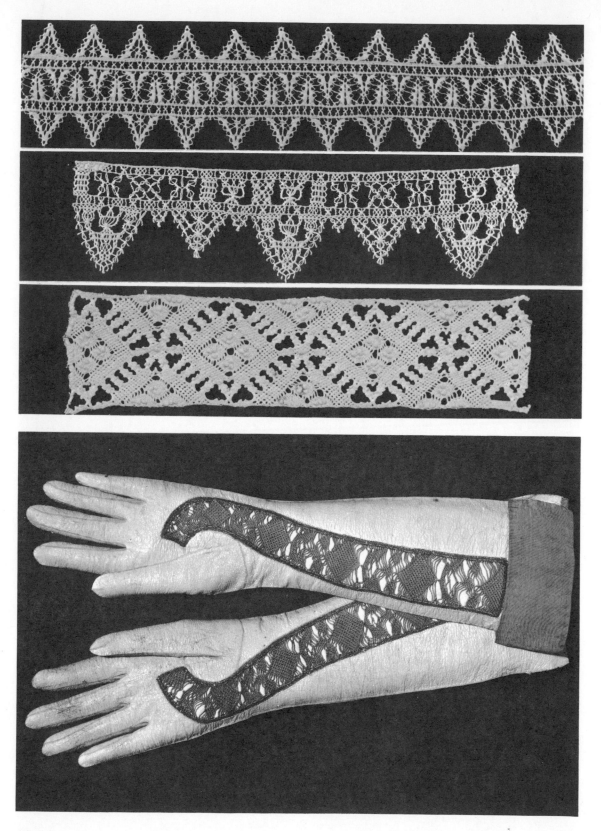

class distinction: the élite made delicate trimmings for tablecloths and other linen; the peasants of Rome made knotted borders for scarves to wear over their heads.

The popularity of knotted lace spread rapidly northward through Europe. Queen Mary, the Dutch-born wife of William of Orange, is believed to have introduced the craft to England in the 17th century. Knotting in fact was reputed to be her favourite pastime, and she is said to have sat for many hours every day at her knotted fringes. Sir Charles Sedley, a notorious court satirist and poet, called her the royal knotter, ridiculed her 'homely habits' and wrote a derisive verse about the queen in which are the lines: 'when she rides in coach abroad, is always knotting threads.'

Her biographer Bishop Gilbert Burnet said of her hobby: 'It was a strange thing to see a queen work for so many hours a day.'

Mary's addiction to knotting may have had bearing in her apparent passion for laces of all kinds. Her lace bill for the year 1694, according to court records, amounted to the enormous sum of £1,918. But by all accounts her husband, William, was even more extravagant with the same commodity. His annual bill for lace with which to trim 'assorted cravats, handkerchieves, combing and barbing cloths', once totalled £2,459!

Knotting again became a royal pastime in the late Georgian era, when Queen Charlotte, wife of George III, was reputed to be an enthusiastic exponent of the craft. In drawing-rooms throughout the country knotting became a favourite occupation for candlelit evenings when the light was too poor for any other form of needlework.

Some fine work was produced during this period, including knotted trimmings on costume and fashion accessories. The kid gloves with knotted insert worked in silk, illustrated opposite, date from this time.

## Origin of the name

The word 'macramé' first came into use around the mid 19th century. It is not – as

*Opposite, top: three 17th century Italian borders in macramé lace – all are very fine and intricately knotted. Below: elbow-length white kid gloves, with a macramé insert in blue silk, made in England in the mid 18th century.*

might be imagined – a French word, but is thought to be derived from the Arabic word *migramah*, which literally means a protection, and hence has come to mean a veil, kerchief or shawl to protect the head.

An alternative theory is that the name might have been derived from the Turkish word, *makrama*, meaning a fringed napkin. One source – mistakenly, I am sure – suggests that the name was taken from an Italian village on the banks of the River Macra where the work was popular. Nevertheless it was in Italy that the name macramé, or sometimes macrami, was first adopted so there might be an element of truth in this story. In France the work was known as *filet de carnasière*.

In its early form the word macramé was used as a noun to denote the homespun huckaback towels with plain fringed edges made at that time in Genoa. Gradually the name came to be applied to the fringes themselves and eventually to the knotting patterns which were evolved and which were totally different in style from the fine Renaissance knotted laces.

During the 19th century macramé was taught in schools and convents along the Riviera, for the simplicity of the craft meant it could be quickly mastered by even very young children.

Mrs. Bury Palliser, in her comprehensive book 'The History of Lace', published towards the end of the 19th century, writes of the macramé being taught in these schools: 'There exists a beautiful and ingenious work taught in the schools and convents along the Riviera. It is carried to a great perfection at Chiavari and also at the Albergo de' Poveri, at Genoa. You see it at every stage. It is almost the first employment of the fingers which the poor children of either sex learn.'

The designs worked at this time however were on the whole simple ones, until in 1843 a richly ornamented piece of old *punto a gropo* was brought to the school at Albergo de' Poveri by the Baroness d'Asti, and Marie Picchetti, a young pupil at the school, had the patience to unpick the fringe and discover how the knots were formed.

From then on the children's work grew more ambitious, the older children inventing new and beautiful patterns. Some of the work was used for church decoration, many items were sold locally, others were exported to South America and to California.

Interest in the craft spread rapidly, and specimens of elaborate macramé work were in the Paris Exhibition of 1867. A Genoese lady's trousseau of the period was not considered complete unless she had undergarments trimmed with macramé knotting.

Meanwhile the sailors had been playing their part in taking the craft to other lands. French sailors introduced it to the east coast Indians of Canada; Spanish sailors took it to Mexico, where it was known as Mexican lace.

No doubt the sailors still considered decorative knotting to be very much their 'invention'. Although the work is known in nautical circles as macramé, it is also sometimes referred to as McNamara's lace. Whether this is derived from the word macramé, or from a seafaring gentleman by the name of McNamara, who was once a skilled exponent of the art, is not known!

### The Victorian era – heyday of macramé

The craft had continued to enjoy a quiet popularity in England but it was not until the late Victorian era that the work suddenly became widely acclaimed. In fact the rise to popularity was so sudden and so dramatic that many people believed it to be a newly-invented craft.

Overdecorated and highly ornamented homes were in vogue and a macramé trimming could further gild the already well-enriched lily. Tasselled knotted borders and fringes were used to edge mantelpieces, shelves, brackets, even four-poster beds.

A woman's place, in this era, was very much in the home, and as servants were cheap and plentiful, the lady of the house frequently had an excess of time on her hands, so she indulged in all forms of decorative – and mainly useless – needlework. To the servants was delegated the humdrum task of 'plain' sewing, the darning and the dressmaking.

Macramé became all the rage for it answered every purpose: it was easy to do, occupied the long leisure hours, and was superbly effective in adding ornamentation to the home.

A needlework magazine of the time

*A Victorian baby's bonnet in a heavy linen thread. Ribbons are threaded through knotting.*

suggested macramé fringes could be used for table and mantel borders, brackets, insertions for antimacassars, nightdress cases, handkerchief sachets, pin cushions, wall pockets and workbags.

A whole new industry sprang into being as special yarns and elaborate equipment and accessories were produced. Many firms were established to produce frames on which to work. Others made bobbins to hold working threads, clamps to support knotting. Books and magazines on the subject flooded the market.

In France and Germany the work was enjoying a similar popularity, and many pattern books were published in these countries. Some of these old books filled with fascinating patterns, are still to be found in second-hand bookshops, and are well worth acquiring. Although the text may be in French or German once the art of macramé has been mastered, the patterns are very easy to 'read' and to copy.

Some of the frames patented in England had ingenious levers and screws on them for holding horizontal cords, and some even had clips fitted to keep knot-bearing cords taut.

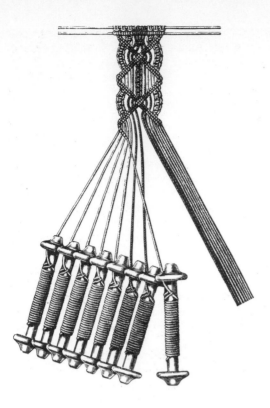

Most of the equipment produced although useful was mainly superfluous, for one of the supreme attractions of macramé is that it requires no special tools or equipment. By the dearth of examples of Victorian knotting boards to be found nowadays, it would seem Victorian ladies thought so too! Magazines of the period offered advice on contriving suitable working surfaces at home.

Weldon's Practical Needlework suggested the following elaborate but no doubt effective base: 'Procure a piece of strong unbleached calico, and make a bag about 18 in. or 20 in. long and 8 in. wide, stuff this firmly with bran and place it in a shallow box of corresponding size which must be heavily

*Left: facsimile of bobbins made during the Victorian era to hold macramé cords. Below: a table runner with macramé insert and knotted fringe. Insert is worked in close cording to represent human figures.*

weighted with lead or sand. The bag should stand an inch above the level of the box, and be covered on the top with bright ingrain cashmere or cloth.'

The bone or ivory fish bobbins made originally in the late Georgian era were revived and new straight-sided bobbins produced (see illustration on page 15). Again these were not generally used and many of the fish bobbins found their way into card counter boxes. A number of them still remain in such places today, their original use unknown or long forgotten.

Excellent macramé threads in good colours and textures were manufactured around this time. And such was the popularity of macramé that a particular form of crochet was evolved, known as crochet macramé – this was simply crochet worked with the thread currently being sold for macramé work. Rather the reverse of the present trend where we use crochet yarns for macramé knotting!

## A new look for an old craft

When the Victorian period ended, and over-elaborate decoration was replaced by the austerity of the 1920s and 30s, macramé too faded from the scene, along with the shell and bead pictures, and the florid embroideries.

In Italy however, in the early part of the 20th century, a particular form of macramé work was evolved by a Madame Valentina Cavandoli. Madame Cavandoli was head of the Casa del Sole, an open-air school in Turin, and she devised a version of macramé based on the wampum weaving principle, and on cross stitch in embroidery to amuse and occupy the children in her care.

The work, now known as Cavandoli work, is knotted in close horizontal and vertical cording in two colours, one for the background, and one for the design. The technique is particularly suitable for all forms of geometric shapes and stylised figures, and the finished effect is of a closely woven fabric, similar in appearance to tapestry. Again, because of the simplicity of the technique, it could be done by even the youngest pupils – boys and girls from the age of five years upwards – and it could be done out-of-doors.

In the 1940s macramé enjoyed a very brief revival on both sides of the Atlantic.

In fact a book on lace-making written around this time states that macramé threads were available in abundance, and in plentiful colours – so the hobby must indeed have been popular.

Despite this, little evidence can be found today of work done during this time. Perhaps as with so much else during the astringency of the wartime and post-war period, the work was shoddy and inexpert, and has long since been banished to attics and old trunks, destined to remain there unseen for several decades at least.

It is only during the last few years that macramé has again been re-discovered, and is now enjoying a welcome and well-deserved return to popularity. One of the many fascinating aspects of this craft is that although the basic knots used in the work have not in any way altered since very early times, the examples from each period of its history and from each part of the world display a vastly different character.

The fine knotted laces of Renaissance Italy, for example, are quite different from the heavy tasselled borders of Victorian England, and different again from the rich fringes of Morocco – see, for instance, the Moroccan panel illustrated on page 35, and compare it with some of the Victorian work illustrated on pages 14, 24 and 118.

And so it is today: modern macramé while still using the same knots, and in similar pattern arrangements, reflects contemporary trends in fashion and design, the flavour of our way of life. Just as our primitive ancestors knotted ropes with whatever materials they had to hand, so today we work our decorative knotting in the materials available to us.

This includes as well as the range of traditional threads whose qualities have long been known and appreciated, many exciting and colourful man-made fibres, and synthetic yarns. And these extend the scope of macramé work far beyond the bounds of possibility ever dreamed of by our grandmothers when they sat at their knotting boards.

Macramé today is accepted as an art form

*Opposite, top: a beautiful bag made in Italy in the early part of the 20th century – the tapestry-like panel round top of bag is a perfect example of Cavandoli work. Below: selection of yarns and other materials suitable for macramé.*

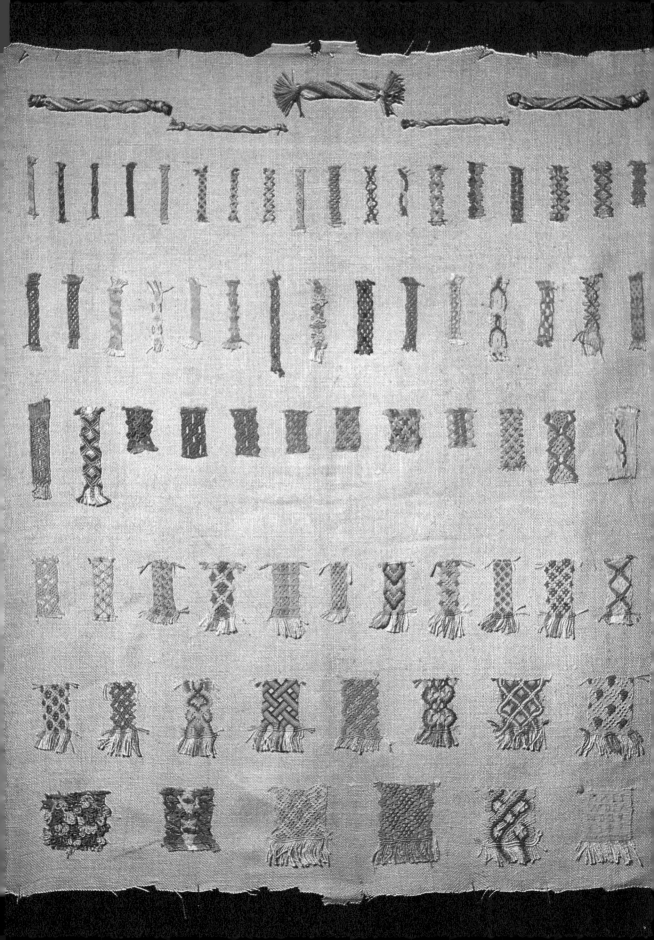

*Opposite: a rare and beautiful sampler of macramé, dated 1749, from the Victoria and Albert Museum collection. Seventy-five tiny macramé pieces have been mounted together — the samples are worked in silk and metal threads in multi-coloured geometric patterns. Below: by contrast, modern macramé in the shape of three knotted sculptures worked in polypropylene and other synthetic ropes.*

in its own right, and is being taught in art colleges, night schools and other educational institutions. To an age-old craft we are contributing all the resources of modern materials and ideas.

Fine intricate work can still be done, as it was in Italy in the 16th century, but at the other end of the scale so can free-standing knotted rope sculptures which are no less beautiful but merely symbolic of the present day. And this is just as it should be. Macramé is the most personal of crafts. It can be all things to all people. How many other crafts can claim this?

# Tools of the trade

Macramé requires the absolute minimum of special equipment: basically all you need to start work is some yarn – and your own fingers! And the yarn can take any form, from the finest knitting or crochet cotton to extra-thick rug wool, from fishing line to ordinary parcel string. Anything will do. Half the fun of macramé comes from experimenting with unusual yarns and materials.

Of course there are many other useful 'accessories' which will help to make working easier for you: a board on which to rest your knotting, for instance, is almost an essential although sometimes – when working 'in the round', or on a three-dimensional hanging or sculpture – a board would only be an encumbrance.

The following list gives suggestions for materials and equipment which you might find useful. Nearly all are normal everyday household items you are likely to have in your home already. Some items you will find of more value than others, depending on the sort of work you aim to do – if you do not intend, for example, to work out your own designs, then you will probably not need graph paper. Also, as you go along you will most likely adapt items yourself to help you with your work – items I have not even thought of.

Macramé is the most personal of handicrafts, and because so few pieces of manufactured equipment are needed it is inevitable that everyone who tries it will adopt his or her own methods. I have, for example, a most useful squat-shaped vase which when turned upside down and padded with foam plastic makes a perfect base for working in the round. Naturally I hesitate to include a vase in my list!

## Essential materials

Yarns (see detailed note, page 22).
Knotting board (see detailed note, page 24).
Pins – preferably glass-headed or 'T' pins. These are used to pin your work to the board and as knotting progresses they will help to shape and regularise the knotting pattern. They will also keep holding and leader cords taut. For big pieces of work, and heavy yarns, indicator pins – sold by office supply shops – are ideal.
Scissors.
Darning needle – to weave in loose ends to the back of your work and so conceal them.

## Useful materials

The following are not essential but useful to have:
Crochet hook and knitting needles – to help pull threads through in complicated knots, or to set cords directly on to a knitted, crocheted or fabric edge.
Tape measure and/or steel ruler – preferably with inches and millimetre markings.
Pencil and notebook – to keep a record of yarns and patterns used. As your work becomes more ambitious, and you start experimenting with different yarns and textures, you will find it essential to keep an accurate record of how each yarn works up. You will also want to jot down ideas for your own designs.
Rubber bands – useful if you are working with long lengths of yarn and need to 'bundle' them to make working easier.
Fabric glue – to use when joining in a new length of yarn by splicing, or for concealing

*Opposite: useful tools and equipment.*

loose ends at the back of work.

Bulldog clip – to clip knotting firmly to the working surface. Useful whenever you want to give extra stability to your work.

Drawing pins – to anchor holding cords to your working surface.

Graph paper – if you intend to plot your own colour designs.

Lace bobbins – again useful if you are working with long ends. In Georgian times little fish-shaped bobbins were made specially to hold macramé working threads. A few of these may still be found in second-hand shops, or you may even have some in your own workbox but have never known what they were for! After the decline of interest in macramé at the turn of the century, many of these bobbins found their way into card counter boxes. Any type

of narrow small spool would do instead of the genuine article – even those from a sewing machine. Or cardboard cut into suitable sized rectangular strips will serve the same purpose, although less decoratively!

Self-adhesive transparent tape – again useful for keeping work in place, concealing loose ends, and so on. Coloured opaque self-adhesive tape can in fact be used as a special feature by binding edges with it. Choose a colour to tone or contrast with the macramé yarn.

Beads and pearls of all kinds, shapes and sizes – if you intend working on designs with this sort of ornamentation.

Any other haberdashery oddments such as buckles, buttons, old brooches, raffia, decorative clasps and so on – gradually

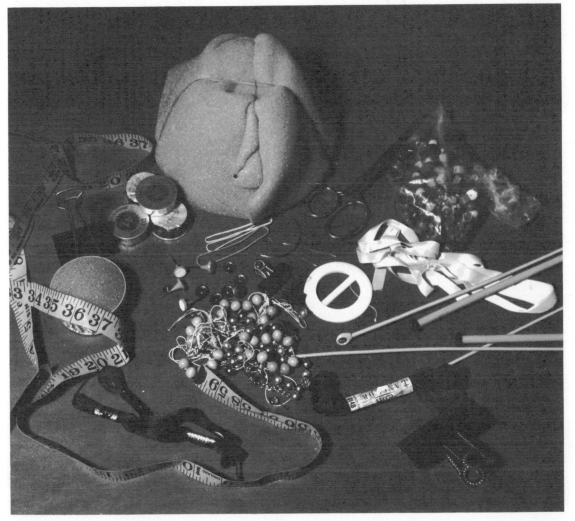

*Assorted sinnets of flat knots. From left to right they are: fine cotton, rayon, fine nylon cord, plastic-coated string, macramé twine, jewelled novelty knitting yarn, piping cord no. 1, double knitting wool, gardening twine, parcel string, medium crochet cotton, novelty metal thread, multi-coloured string, synthetic tubular cord, raffia, piping cord no. 5, extra thick Orlon, fishing line.*

build up a stock of decorative items. Even sea shells, feathers, and lengths of copper piping can come in useful!

## YARNS

Originally macramé was worked in one type of yarn only. This was a smooth linen twine which was available in many thicknesses but only in the one shade: a natural, typically string shade of beige. Purists still insist this is the only yarn that should ever be used for macramé work, but this book is designed to show how an old craft can be adapted effectively and attractively to reflect modern trends, and although a genuine macramé yarn is a joy to work with because it knots smoothly and is pleasant to handle, your work would be greatly limited if you never tried any other yarn. Nevertheless it is worth making efforts to track down a quantity of proper macramé yarn just to enjoy the pleasure of working with it. It looks exactly like fine string – and in fact a ball of ordinary twine can be used instead if the real thing cannot be located.

However much of the satisfaction of

macramé work comes from experimenting, discovering new and different yarns, and achieving unusual effects often by combining several yarn types. Nothing is barred: everything from thick upholstery cord to the finest silk may be used, from sturdy garden twines to marine ropes, from plastic-coated string to spiky metal threads . . .

This is the joy of macramé: with knitting or crochet you are usually limited to one or two similar yarns to produce a particular pattern; not so with macramé – by working the same pattern in a variety of separate yarns, astonishingly different results can be achieved. The illustration above, left, shows a chain of flat knots worked in a variety of yarns – you will see for yourself how one chain differs dramatically from the next.

Before you dash out to buy a mass of assorted strings and yarns however there are several important points to take into consideration:

**Wearing qualities.** Naturally some yarns wear much better than others and this should be taken into account when you select yarn for a particular project. A fine soft wool, for

*Some strings, twines and cords.*

instance, would not be right for an everyday handbag, although combined with a strong metal thread could be effective for an evening bag which would not be subjected to so much wear and tear. And while a cobwebby cotton will look lovely for a lacy table mat, you will want something a bit sturdier and more substantial for a lampshade, say, or a cushion cover.

**Colour.** The yarns which knot most successfully are often, unfortunately, those which come in the most limited range of colours. Piping cord for instance which is available in a multitude of thicknesses and which knots well is invariably sold only in white. Dishcloth cotton which is also a good knotting yarn, and softer than piping cord, although sometimes available in a small range of colours, is more

often than not only to be found in white or a natural shade. Dyeing is one answer (see page 139), but if it's colour rather than texture you want then the answer is to use knitting yarns – real or synthetic – which come in all manner of thicknesses and colours. Twines too nowadays are being produced in an increasing range of colours, and sometimes two or three shades are combined in the one ball. These will give a pleasant multi-coloured look to your work. Rug wool and synthetic cording are available in good colour ranges.

**Texture.** Again an important consideration. If you want a crisp finish with the knotting pattern clearly visible then it is best to stick to the twines and smooth linen and cotton yarns which knot easily and keep their shape. On the other hand if you want a pleasing textural effect where the actual knots are not so important then wool – fine or thick – should be the choice. There are many interesting novelty yarns available nowadays which are worth trying – there is even one which gives the impression of fur.

**Sources of supply.** Almost anywhere – once you begin to look – will provide a source of supply for yarns. The obvious places to begin the hunt are the wool and haberdashery counters where all types of knitting and crochet yarns and cordings are sold. Good strong linen threads can be found in upholstery and hardware departments. Theatrical supply shops often have an unusual and rewarding range of novelty yarns and cords. Marine stores will provide strong nautical ropes, natural and synthetic, and gardening stores and stationers have twine in various thicknesses, types and colours. Hobby and craft shops are worth a visit, not only for yarns but for beads and other decorative accessories.

You will soon learn to be constantly on the look out for unusual yarns, and will learn too to recognise the particular advantages and disadvantages of each and how these characteristics can be utilised to best effect in your work: nylon yarns, for instance, tend to slip when knotted, and wools do not hold their shape well unless mounted on a fabric lining. Some yarns will 'bulk' up much more than their initial appearance would indicate. Only by constant experimenting and keeping an accurate record of your findings will you gradually discover what's right for what purpose.

Sometimes yarns can have their plies unwound and each strand used separately (the run shown on page 112 was made from unplied extra thick piping cord).

### Some yarns to try

All cotton yarns – from the finest to the thickest
All twines – gardening, marine and household
Piping cord
Dishcloth cotton
Cording – natural and synthetic
Upholstery thread
Raffia
Knitting and crochet yarns – natural and synthetic
Rug wool
Novelty yarns – such as glitter threads, metal threads, bobble wool
Plastic-coated twine
Fine ribbon
Hemp
Jute
Sisal
Paper cellophane

## WORKING SURFACES

Although macramé knotting boards have been manufactured in the past, especially in Victorian times, I do not know of any which are made nowadays. You could be lucky enough to find an old board in a second-hand shop, but these are few and far between.

The reason for this dearth of boards is most likely due to the fact that even in Victorian days it was a simple matter to construct a knotting board at home, and to improvise with whatever materials came to hand, so there was probably little demand for a ready-made board. Some of the Victorian boards had clips fitted to hold knot-bearing cords taut, and knobs down the sides on which to anchor holding and leader cords. Of course such fittings are useful but the effect can be achieved just as well with drawing or 'T' pins. Also one knotting board would not necessarily answer every purpose. If you are working on a large piece of macramé, you would – naturally – need a board to fit; conversely if you are working on a tiny item a large board would only be cumbersome.

The important thing about your board is that it should give adequate support to your work, yet its surface should be soft enough to take pins, and the thickness sufficient to prevent the pins coming through to the other side and causing unnecessary damage to you!

The piece of Victorian knotting pictured below is mounted on a block of fairly hard untreated wood. Normally such wood would be too hard to take pins, but as this work has each of its leader cords bound tightly right round the board three times, the need for pinning is obviated so the wood provides an excellent firm working surface.

The best size of working surface to practise on is approximately 18 in. by 12 in.

*Opposite: Victorian knotting on a board. Leader cords are wound round board to anchor work.*

Try any of the following materials:

Plastic foam — buy it in sheets from hardware stores. One sheet is unlikely to be thick enough so either use three or four thicknesses together, or else mount one sheet on to a wood or firm card backing.

Towelling (several thicknesses) is a good soft yet firm surface as an alternative to plastic, and can be attached to the top of a wooden or card board with a bulldog clip. Candlewick and felt are also suitable.

Any reasonably soft wood, cut to suitable size — fibreboard is excellent.

Cork makes an ideal board for it takes pins easily, also you can pencil guide marks on it when required. An old bath mat (hard to find nowadays as most of the modern mats are plastic!) is just right. Or you can buy self-adhesive cork tiles — again several together will be required to give a reasonable thickness.

Weighted pillow — this is based on another favourite Victorian method (see picture on page 26). A sand-stuffed cushion or pillow containing a heavy weight to stabilise it makes an excellent surface for pinning. In Caulfeild and Saward's Dictionary of Needlework, published at the turn of the century, it was suggested that *'the Cushion should be an oblong flat-shaped pillow, 12 in. long by 8 in. wide, stuffed with sand, or otherwise weighted, and covered with a good Ticking; arrange the lines woven in the Ticking evenly along the length of the Cushion, as they can be used as guides for the horizontal lines of the work.'* The idea is still a sound one, and as ticking can be bought from soft furnishing departments by the yard you can easily construct your own Victorian-

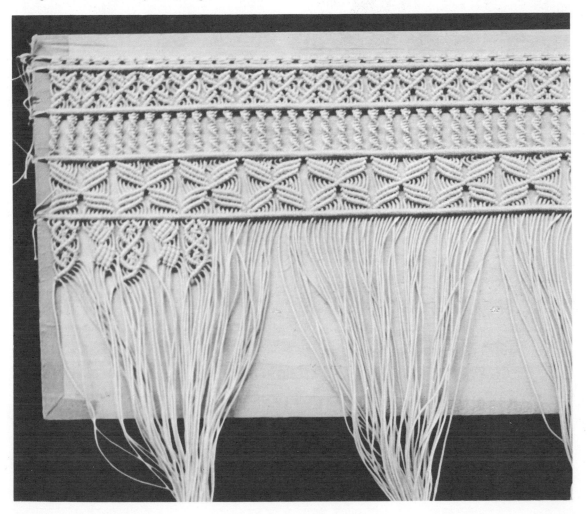

style macramé cushion.

Cardboard – again several thicknesses and preferably with a soft padded top (plastic foam, towelling or candlewick).

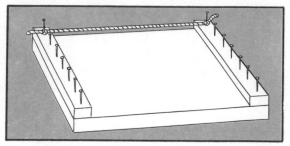

If you wish to construct a rather more superior board the sketch above shows one idea, based on the Victorian models with pegs at the sides and top.

For large pieces of work where a board is out of the question, a wall surface, or the back of a door, preferably covered with stick-on cork tiles works well. Big hooks can be inserted at the sides at intervals all the way up, then if your work is mounted on a holding rod it can be slotted into the hooks at the most convenient level for you to knot, and moved up as the piece progresses. I am fortunate in having a convenient area of unused wall in my kitchen just right for working on large items. I can then knot between washing-up, feeding the dog, cooking the supper, or any other domestic pursuit! Every time I pass the wall I automatically stop and tie another knot – this way the work soon grows.

Alternatively, an artist's easel, if you have one, or even a music stand can give support for big pieces of work.

A dressmaker's dummy is – naturally – an ideal base when making garments.

For work where pinning is not so vital, a fairly simple frame can be constructed from a wooden box and clamps.

A weaver's warping board, with a pair of pegs placed at the appropriate distance apart, can also give a good working base.

Two chairs placed at a suitable distance apart

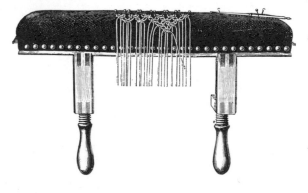

*Top left: an oddment of any soft wood can be used as a base for your first practise samplers.*
*Below: facsimile of an elaborate padded cushion made in Victorian days as a macramé base.*

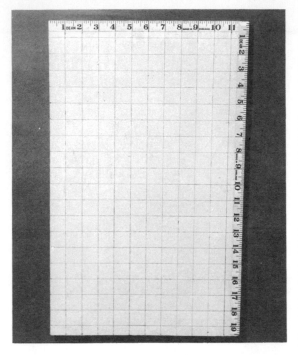

*It is worth taking time and trouble to prepare your board by marking it into inch squares.*

*A page from an art student's notebook, recording an idea for a macramé-patterned dress.*

will do the same job, for work can be suspended between knobs on the backs of the chairs, or pinned to the chairs.

Other suitable ideas: two adjacent drawers in which either end of the work can be wedged; two clamps from a table tennis set fixed to a table surface a suitable distance apart; a child's pegboard.

An ironing board is a good surface when pinning out intricate knots but obviously is not suitable for everyday use.

My own extremely makeshift but all-purpose knotting board is constructed from a sheet of plastic foam and a cardboard box. The plastic is backed on to one side of the box and wedged into the lid. It is a handy-sized lightweight portable board and ideal for most purposes. Its major disadvantage is that I cannot mark guide lines on the working surface. When guide lines are required, or when I want a larger and more substantial base I use a sheet of fibreboard. As fibreboard is available with one side already whitened, this is ideal for marking out with squares and other guide lines.

## If you are working in the round

Circular work and three-dimensional designs need a firm base in the centre. A suitable shaped wooden block would do, or an upturned vase, jam jar or glass tumbler preferably padded with plastic foam or towelling so you may pin knots as you work. See other ideas on page 96.

## To prepare your board

A section of tape measure glued along the top and down one side of your working board gives a useful at-a-glance guide to measurements; and marking the surface of the board into 1-in. squares provides the basis for most guide lines. These should be marked with an indelible pen or pencil. When specific guide lines are required for a particular pattern they can be pencilled lightly on top of the 1-in. grid, and rubbed out afterwards. The indelible grid provides a permanent and extremely valuable guide.

A wood, cork or cardboard working surface can have grids and guide lines drawn on them direct but plastic foam would have to be first covered with a thin sheet of card.

## KEEPING A RECORD

As macramé is so much a matter of experi-

27

ment and personal preference, it is essential right from the beginning that you keep a record of your work, and the yarns you use. A notebook, preferably with a stiff cover as it will probably have to withstand constant wear and tear, should be kept exclusively for this purpose.

It is best to divide the book into three distinct parts, each dealing in turn with yarns, patterns and design notes.

Each time you use a particular yarn, note down in the first part of your book any remarks relevant to the yarn – e.g. how it knots, whether it keeps its knot firmly, or is inclined to slip, if it makes up quickly, or is fiddly to work with. Add to this the price and where you purchased it, and if other colours and thicknesses are available.

In the second section of the book keep a record of every item you make up, whether from a pattern you yourself have created, or one from a book or magazine. A brief outline or sketch of the pattern should be indicated, sufficient to remind you of what it was, with knot detail added if required. Then beside it a note of the yarn you used to make it up, and the quantity required.

The last section of the book would record your own design ideas – and once you are a confirmed macramé exponent, you will find these ideas come thick and fast. Practically anything can spark off an idea: the wrought iron railing round a building, a pattern created by light through trees, a printed design on fabric, a carving on a building ... As soon as the idea comes it is best to record it immediately before inspiration goes!

In the design section too you can plan colour charts for work in two or more colours – it is helpful here to have a few pages of graph paper inserted in your notebook.

All in all, taking the trouble to keep a record of your work will pay dividends in the long run. Who knows, you might even publish your notebook one day!

## WHERE TO WORK

One of the many appealing aspects of macramé is that it can be done almost anywhere. Ideally of course it should be done in a good light, and a comfortable place. If you are working on a particularly large item then obviously your choice of working area will be limited, but small items mounted on a portable lightweight board can be conveniently carried around with you to do on train journeys, in waiting-rooms, sitting in a park or on a beach, and at any odd moment during the day when you have a few minutes to spare. Knotting can also be comfortably done on your lap while you are sitting watching television.

*Magnificent Chinese banner, late 19th century, which has a macramé fringe – flat knot sinnets with picots, and Turk's heads above tassels.*

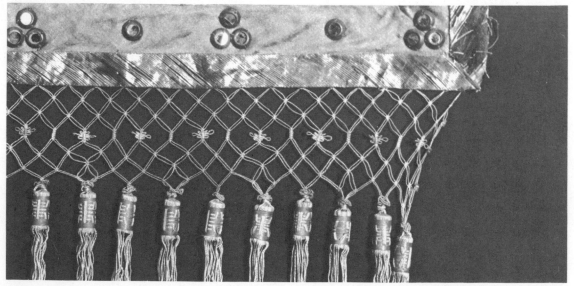

# Starting work

## SETTING ON THREADS

Before you can begin knotting, it is necessary to cut the yarn into suitable lengths and then mount these cut ends in one of several ways so you have a firm basis for working.

Threads can be mounted on a length of yarn (the same as the working threads or a yarn of a contrasting colour, texture or thickness), or on any sort of rigid support such as a slim knitting needle (pointed at both ends), a glass stirring rod, a wooden pole, length of cane, or even a drinking straw. If you are adding a fringe or border to an existing item then the knotting threads are mounted directly on to the fabric. This process of mounting is called **setting on threads.** If threads are set on to a length of yarn this yarn is called the **holding cord.**

Normally knotting is done on two threads, four threads, or any multiple of two or four, so inevitably the total number of threads required is going to be an even number — there are occasions where an odd number is required as you will see in due course, but these are not so common. Therefore as the even number is the more usual event, when threads are mounted they are cut singly then doubled. When you work a specific pattern the instructions will usually tell you to cut so many lengths of yarn, and these are the actual lengths of yarn you cut. When they are doubled and set on, you will of course have twice as many working ends. For example, a pattern may tell you to cut 12 threads, each 4 ft. long. When these 12 threads are set on to a holding cord, you will have 24 working ends, each 2 ft. long.

*It is important always to remember when cutting threads that you cut to double the measurement required for each knotting end.*

*Setting on threads—to a fabric edge (top); to a holding cord (left); to a rod (right).*

There are other methods of setting on threads but for the moment only the basic methods will be explained — the others will follow later.

### Setting on to a holding cord

Sometimes the holding cord will be used to form part of the design in which case a pattern will instruct you to cut the holding cord to a particular length. Normally however it is used only as a foundation on which to set on working threads and it is either withdrawn when work is complete, or the ends concealed at the back of the work. It should be long enough to hold the number of set-on threads comfortably with sufficient length left at either side to tie round a pin which is then anchored to your knotting surface.

As a rough guide, if you cut your holding cord to 6 in. longer than the total finished width of the item you are making, this should be adequate. Threads are mounted centrally on the holding cord, leaving 3 in. either side.

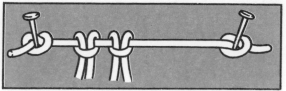

Near one end of the holding cord form a loop. Wrap the cord round itself and pull the end through the loop. This is known as an **overhand knot.**

Position the knot (before pulling it tightly) on your knotting surface and insert a pin through the centre of knot. Tighten the knot around pin so it is firmly anchored to the board.

A similar knot is tied at the other end of the holding cord, and secured to your working surface. You are now ready to set on threads.

There are various ways of setting on threads to give a decorative beginning to your work. Instructions for these are given in a later section. For the moment we will deal only with a simple plain mounting.

Some people prefer to set on threads before mounting the holding cord on to a working surface, while others use the method given above which is to mount both ends of the cord, and then set threads on over the already taut holding cord. Personally I find it easiest to mount one end of the cord only, then set on threads, and then mount the other end of the holding cord. Whichever method you use, it is essential that the holding cord is pulled taut otherwise your work will sag in the middle.

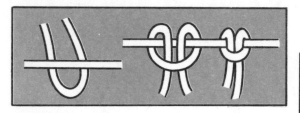

For practising purposes, cut 8 threads, each 4 ft. long. Take one thread, double it and insert looped end under holding cord, from top to bottom.

Bring the 2 loose ends down over the holding cord and through the loop. Pull them to tighten loop on holding cord. This is called mounting with a **reversed double half hitch** or, alternatively, it is sometimes known as the lark's head, or cow hitch. Throughout this book it will be referred to as the reversed double half hitch.

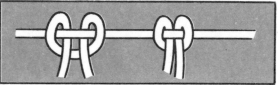

Sometimes it is preferred not to have the knot of the reversed double half hitch showing on the front of your work. In this case threads can be set on in reverse – i.e. place looped end of thread under holding cord from bottom to top, fold down over holding cord and take loose ends through loop. Tighten round holding cord as before.

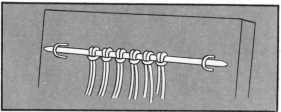

**Setting threads on to a rod**

To set threads on to any rigid holding line follow instructions for mounting on to a holding cord, but secure rod to your working surface with 'U' pins or staples.

Continue mounting remaining threads in the same way. Position each set of threads close to the previous one, so there is no unnecessary space between the knotting ends.

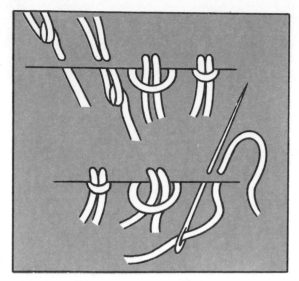

### Setting threads on to fabric

To set threads on for a fringe or other decorative border, the threads should be pulled through the fabric approximately $\frac{1}{4}$ in. from the edge, in a similar way to setting on to a holding cord. On a knitted, crocheted or any loose-weave fabric, a crochet hook can be used to pull loop end of doubled thread through the fabric. On a close-woven fabric, the yarn should be threaded on to a large-eyed darning needle and 'sewn' through the edge. In every method thread ends are pulled through loop so the thread appears to have been set on with a reversed double half hitch. See also page 130.

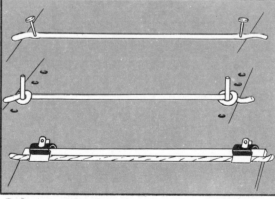

### Other methods of mounting holding cord

The ends can be secured firmly to a board or table with drawing pins or 'T' pins, taking the pins through cord without using overhand knots.

If using a warping board, chair back or other form of protruding pegs or knobs as a working basis merely knot cord ends firmly round the anchors.

Further support to work can be given by securing holding cord and set-on threads to the top of working board with a bulldog clip.

### THE BASIC KNOTS

Surprising as it may seem when you look at examples of finished macramé work the entire technique of macramé knotting is based on two very simple knots. There are almost limitless permutations of these two knots, such as the Japanese and the mous variety of attractive patterns and finished effects. Also, some more complex knots, such as the Japanese and the Josephine, which are derived from the basic knots have earned their own names so as they may be more easily identifiable. These will be described in due course — but first the basic knots.

The **half hitch** is worked with two cords (or multiples thereof); the **flat knot** needs a minimum of four cords, but it can in fact be worked with a multiple of four or, as you will see, any number at all.

When the half hitch is worked twice it is called the **double half hitch**, or sometimes the clove hitch. In its single form the knot is sometimes termed the simple knot or buttonhole loop. The flat knot is also known as the square knot, Solomon's knot, the macramé knot or even the sailor's knot.

Throughout this book both basic knots will be referred to as the half hitch and the flat knot respectively.

### Half hitch

This knot can be tied from the left or right. To tie it from the left, the right-hand cord (known as the **knot-bearing cord**) should be held taut, the left-hand cord is brought in front of it, then taken up and under it, the free end being brought through the loop formed and pulled tight. Continue in this way to form a chain.

To work from right to left, the left-hand cord becomes the knot-bearing cord and is held taut. The right-hand cord is then looped over it and pulled tight.

If half hitches are worked alternately from left and right an interesting and useful chain is formed. This chain can be worked with single cords or, if a chunkier effect is wanted, then double cords are used. This is sometimes called the seesaw knot. Whenever a **chain** is referred to in a pattern, it is usually this form of the half hitch worked alternately from the left and right which is intended.

A half hitch chain worked continuously from the same side tends naturally to twist on itself. This can be used to good effect when a twisted chain is wanted. But by gently easing each half hitch as you work it you can persuade the chain to lie flat.

### Simple variations on the half hitch

Once the technique of working the half hitch has been mastered, and the art of producing a regular, even chain lies really in keeping the knot-bearing cord taut at all times, then a few simple variations can be tried.

One of the easiest variations is simply to work half hitches over a central 'core' of two (or more) cords. As these central cords now become the knot-bearers, they must be kept taut while the outer cords are knotted over them. You can if you wish pin

them to your working surface so they remain constantly taut. When a knot is worked over a central core it is often termed a **bar**. But again, as with so much of the terminology used in macramé the application of the word 'bar' seems to vary considerably from one reference source to the other.

**Single Genoese bar** (above, left). Work alternate right and left half hitches over a core of 2 central cords.

**Double Genoese bar** (above, right). Work groups of 2 half hitches alternately from the right and left over a central core of 2 cords.

**Treble Genoese bar** (above, left). Work groups of 3 half hitches alternately from the right and left over a central core of 2 cords.

**Waved bar** (above, right). An unusual, pleasing effect which is another variation on the Genoese bar. Groups of 5 half hitches are worked alternately from the right and left over a central 2-cord core. Alternatively, groups of 7 half hitches can be worked. Groups of any number will in fact create a similar effect but the term 'waved bar' is traditionally only given to the 5 or 7 grouped bars.

**Corkscrew bar.** This variation uses only 3 cord ends: 1 knotting cord, 2 knot-bearers. Work half hitches continuously from one side only. A spiral will gradually be created round the 2 knot-bearers. A **buttonhole bar** is worked the same way but in this the knots are tied looser and eased to lie flat so they do not spiral. Both the corkscrew and the buttonhole bars can be worked from the right or left, as required.

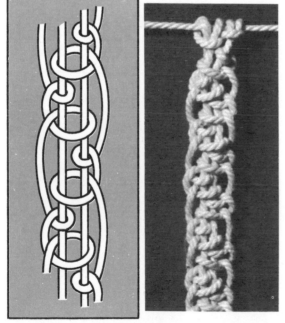

Another alternating pattern on 4 ends: work a half hitch from the right over the right-hand central core cord, then work another half hitch from the right over both central cords. Now work one half hitch from the left over the left-hand central core cord, then a half hitch from the left over both central cords. Repeat the alternating pattern to form a chain.

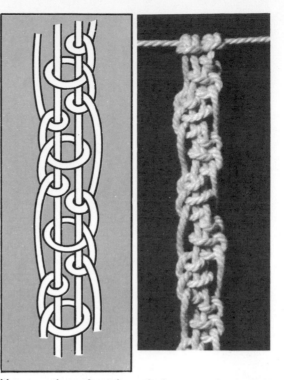

Yet another 4-end variation: work a half hitch from the right over the right-hand central core cord, then work a half hitch from the right over both central cords, then another half hitch from the right over the right-hand central cord only. Repeat knotting sequence from the left: one half hitch over left-hand central cord, one half hitch over both central cords, one half hitch over left hand central cord only. Continue in this way.

These few variations already should be enough to show you the many permutations of knotting sequences and patterns that are available. Try devising your own patterns, by experimenting with different groups of half hitches. Or by working a chain over several central core cords to create a wider and more solid effect.

### Half hitch sampler

**PREPARATION.** Cut 10 threads, each 20 in. long. Double them and mount them with reversed double half hitches on to a holding cord approximately 6 in. long (you now have 20 working ends).

**YARN.** The sampler illustrated is made in a medium-weight cotton twine. The finished work measures 3 in. by 2 in. (plus fringe).

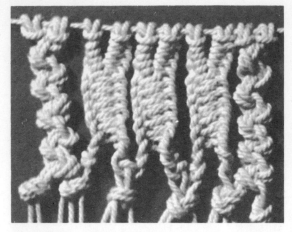

Any strong yarn which produces a tension of 6 loops on the holding cord to 1 in. could be used to achieve a similar finished size. It is often helpful when practising macramé knots and working experimental samplers to use 2 yarns of different colours, providing they are of similar weight and thickness. The colour contrast helps to show you the course of each cord as it is knotted and also helps to prevent cords being knotted out of order.

**TO MAKE.** To simplify instructions, the cords are numbered from 1 to 20 (see diagram below). Use pins to mark off cords into groups of 4.

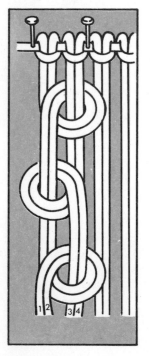

**Work first group of 4**: work a double chain of alternate half hitches with cords 1 and 2, and 3 and 4. Continue until chain is 2 in. long.

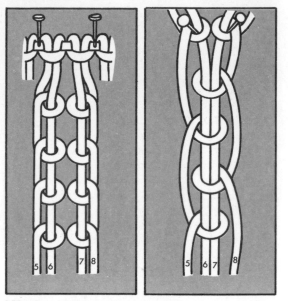

**Work second group of 4**: *work 4 half hitches from the left with cords 5 and 6, easing knots to lie flat; work 4 half hitches from the right with cords 7 and 8, easing knots to lie flat.

Bring the ends of these 2 chains together (pin them to the working surface if necessary to keep them in place). Cords 6 and 7 now become the central knot-bearing core. Work alternate half hitches from the right and left with cords 5 and 8 over the central core. When you have worked 6 half hitches from each side (i.e. 12 half hitches altogether), pin the bottom of chain to working surface to keep it steady, and divide cords into 2 pairs again.

Work 4 half hitches from the left with cords 5 and 6, easing knots to lie flat; work 4 half hitches from the right with cords 7 and 8, easing knots to lie flat.** Repeat from * to ** for cords 9, 10, 11 and 12, and then for cords 13, 14, 15 and 16. Work a double chain of alternate half hitches with cords 17 and 18, and 19 and 20 to match the first chain worked on cords 1, 2, 3 and 4.

*Opposite, top: a macramé panel from Morocco, late 19th century, in heavy silk cords, worked mainly in true lover's knots. Below: part of a Chinese overskirt, also 19th century, with a macramé fringe in coloured silks.*

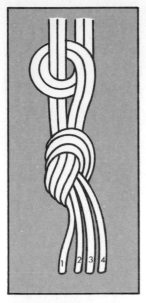

**TO FINISH.** Tie an overhand knot at the bottom of each chain.

### Flat knot

The second basic knot is the flat knot which is formed by tying two **half knots**. A minimum of four cords is required: the two outside cords are used to tie the knot, the two inner ones form the central knot-bearing core.

When working half and flat knots it is important to keep the central knot-bearing cords as taut as possible. You may find it sufficient to loop them firmly round your fingers as you work, or you can pin them to the working surface (provided they are not pinned so tightly as to prevent working cords being passed underneath them). Alternatively, if you are working on a big scale, the core cords can be tied round your waist or tucked into your waistband.

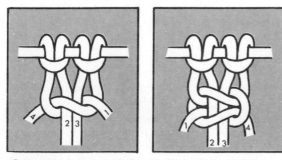

*Opposite: heavy poncho in sisal string. Open-work pattern is in alternate flat knots.*

Keeping centre cords taut, take left-hand cord under the centre core, and over the right-hand cord. Now bring right-hand cord over the centre core and under the left-hand cord. Pull this knot evenly into place over the centre cords, and you have completed a half knot.

To form the flat knot work another half knot but this time work from right to left – i.e. begin by taking right-hand cord under centre core and over left-hand cord, then bring left-hand cord over centre core and under right-hand cord. Draw knot tightly close to the first half knot.

If you continue in this way working flat knots you will form a chain known as **Solomon's bar.**

Flat knots can be started from the left or right: the method above starts from the left, i.e. left-hand cord begins the knotting sequence. To work from right to left, begin with right-hand cord and form first half knot. For the second half knot, begin with left-hand cord.

### Simple variations on the half and flat knots

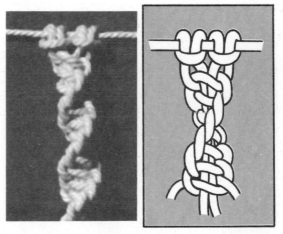

A continuous chain of half knots will produce a twisted spiral. If the half knots are begun each time with the left-hand cord the spiral will twist to the left; if the half knots are begun each time with the right-hand cord the spiral will twist to the right. After about the fourth half knot, the spiral will have twisted right round on itself. Let it twist, so the first and fourth cords have changed positions, and continue to knot.

After every fourth knot let the chain twist and continue to work on the new first and fourth cords.

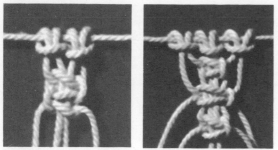

**Triple knot.** Work a flat knot and then a half knot. This creates a firmer knot than a flat knot on its own and is useful when working patterns of alternate flat knots (see below).

**Flat knot on 6 cords.** Work a flat knot on the centre 4 cords, then work a flat knot using 2 outer cords as knotting cords, and the 4 centre cords as a knot-bearing core. To complete knot, work another flat knot on the 4 centre cords.

**Alternate flat knot pattern.** This pattern recurs frequently in all forms of macramé work. It is easy to do, and extremely effective especially when used to create a fabric. Make a simple sampler in an alternate flat knot pattern as follows:

*Above and opposite: bags, ancient and modern, in the alternate flat knot pattern. Modern bag, above, is in parcel string. The two bags opposite are examples of 18th century English work. Both are knotted in cotton cord over a silk lining.*

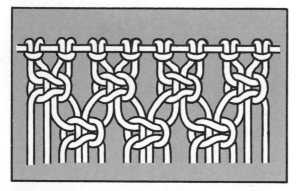

Set on 8 threads each 4 ft. long, on a holding cord (16 working ends, each 2 ft.). Work from left to right throughout.
**1st row**: work flat knots, using 4 cords for each knot.
**2nd row**: leave first 2 cords unworked, then continue across row working flat knots with 4 cords for each knot. Leave final 2 cords unworked.

Repeat first and 2nd rows 6 more times. On odd rows take care not to pull the 2 unworked cords of previous rows at each end too tightly – pinning them to working surface will help to prevent this, and keep the loops regular throughout.
If you pull every knot tight you create a dense fabric. If you leave space between the knots, you create a delicate lacy effect – see the pictures above and opposite.

**Variations on the alternate flat knot pattern**

Work triple knots in an alternate sequence, as for the alternate flat knot sampler left, substituting triple knots for flat knots.

Work alternate sequence of flat knots on 6 cords, by combining 3 cords from each group in the second row, and leaving 3 cords at either end unworked. (**Note.** Cords should be set on in multiples of 6.)

Below left: work 4 flat knots on each group of 4 cords. **5th row**: leave first 2 cords unworked and continue across row working flat knots using 4 cords for each knot. Leave final 2 cords unworked. Repeat 5th row, then repeat 1st–4th rows. Continue in this way with alternate bands of 4-knot Solomon's bars and 2-knot Solomon's bars.

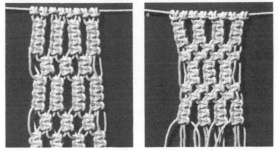

Above right: 3-knot Solomon s bars, 4 cords for each knot. Next work 2 rows of single flat knots, in alternate sequence, then following the alternate sequence from previous row, work another band of 3-knot Colomon's bars. Continue in this way.

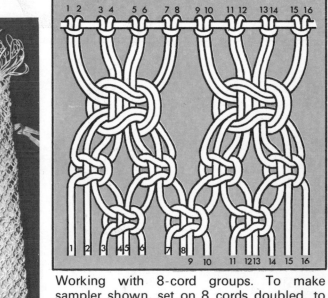

Working with 8-cord groups. To make sampler shown, set on 8 cords doubled, to give 16 working ends. **1st row**: work flat knots, using cords 1 and 2, and 7 and 8 as knotting cords, and tying them over a central core of cords 3, 4, 5 and 6. **2nd row**: separate each group of 8 cords into 2 groups of 4 and work single flat knots right across. **3rd row**: as first row. **4th row**: link the chains by leaving cords 1 and 2 unworked,

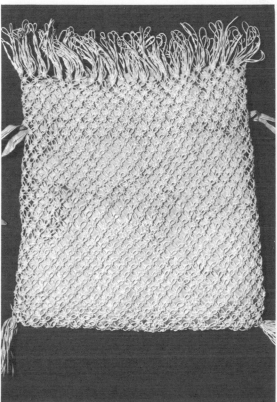

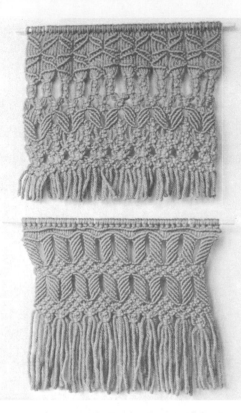

then tying flat knots with each group of 4 ends. Leave cords 15 and 16 unworked.

This is the 4-row pattern. Repeat it until work is desired length.

If this pattern is worked in a strong twine it makes up well for a sturdy shopping bag.

## CORDING

This is another extremely important macramé technique for it is used to create shapes and figures, and to control colour in designs

*Right: samplers in rug wool — cording motifs alternate with flat knots. Below: border worked in heavy waxed string, 19th century — cording motifs, half hitch chains and overhand knots.*

using two or more different coloured yarns. The technique is based on the half hitch knot, and can be used to give vertical, horizontal or diagonal cording as required.

As with the basic half hitch, one cord is used as a knot-bearing cord (or **leader**), another is used to tie the knot. The leader cord can be attached separately by means of pinning to the working surface close to the knotting; or the holding cord can be used provided it has been cut long enough; or one of the set-on cords can be used. For horizontal cording, this would normally be the cord on the far left. For practice purposes it is best to attach a separate leader.

## Horizontal cording

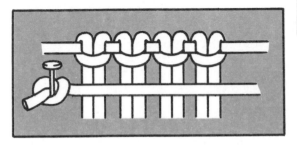

Tie an overhand knot near one end of the leader cord and pin it to working surface to the left of knotting cords and just below the set-on edge. Hold leader in a horizontal position across front of knotting cords. It is important the leader is held as tautly as possible in order to produce an even row of cording. Ideally the leader should be positioned across knotting cords and then anchored to working surface with pins at both sides so you have your hands free to concentrate on the actual knotting.

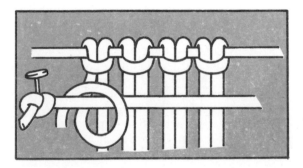

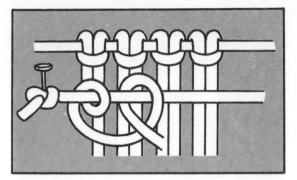

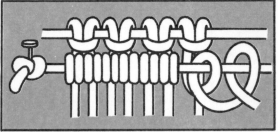

Working from left to right, bring first knotting cord up then pass it behind leader and down through loop formed. Draw knot tight, and repeat it — this forms a **double half hitch**. Continue in this way across the row, working a double half hitch with each knotting cord in turn, and being sure to draw each knot tight against the previous.

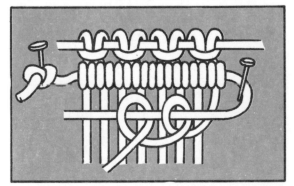

Place a pin in the working surface at the end of the first row, release the leader cord if it has been pinned and reverse its direction, taking it round pin and horizontally across front of work from right to left. Now work double half hitches across row as before, working this time from right to left. At the end of this row, place a pin in working surface as before, and reverse leader cord round it. Continue in this way to produce solid horizontal cording.

## Vertical cording

This differs from horizontal — and also, as you will see, from diagonal — cording in that the leader cord is used to form the knots; the set-on cords become the knot-bearers.

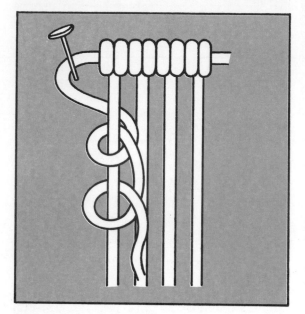

To work vertical cording from left to right, take the knotting cord, which again can be a separate cord pinned to left-hand side of work, or the holding cord, or the first set-on cord, behind first vertical cord, and loop it round the front of the vertical cord then up and back under it. Pull knot tight being sure to keep vertical cord taut all the time. Repeat for 2nd half of the knot.

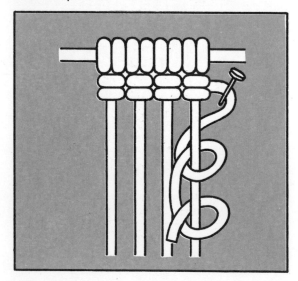

To work vertical cording from right to left, merely reverse the procedure, bringing knotting cord from the right, under the first vertical cord on the right, looping it round and through in the same way. The important thing to remember is always to have the knotting cord pointing in the direction you are working, and also to take it under the knot-bearing cord each time before beginning to tie the knot.

Vertical cording can be worked on one cord only, and this is sometimes used to form a neat side edging for a design. In this case, although you are working on one cord only, you must still work in 'rows' — i.e. work vertical cording once from left to right, then reverse direction of knotting cord and work vertical cording once from right to left, then from left to right, and so on, alternating the direction every time, and pinning knotting cord at the end of each 'row' if necessary. If you attempt to work vertical cording continuously from the same side you will get an uneven and twisted cording which is unattractive.

## Sampler to make

Using horizontal and vertical cording and flat knots

**YARN.** Macramé twine.

**MEASUREMENT.** Finished sampler measures approx. 2 in. by 2½ in., plus fringe.

**PREPARATION.** Cut 9 threads each 3 ft., cut 2 threads each 6 ft. Double them and set them with reversed double half hitches on to a holding cord about 9 in. long, placing the long threads one at each end of row (all the extra length should be in first and last working end, so the second and second-last working ends are of the same length as all other ends). You now have 22 working ends.

**TO MAKE.** Using cord on far left as leader, work a row of horizontal cording right across row. At the end of the row, reverse the direction of the leader round a pin and work a second row of horizontal cording immediately below the first one.

*Leaving the first 3 cords for the moment unworked, tie 4 flat knots; leave the final

## Diagonal cording

This is worked in a similar way to horizontal cording except the leader cord is held at an angle across work and each cord knotted over it in turn. By varying the angle of the leader cord, close diagonal cording can be obtained or an open pattern with areas of unworked cords.

Horizontal and vertical cording are generally used to create solid fabrics, and can be thought of as chiefly functional techniques. Diagonal cording, on the other hand, can be considered the decorative cording technique for it forms the basis for a multitude of fascinating designs. In fact, once the elements of vertical cording have been mastered it is even possible to 'draw' shapes and figures with it (see picture on page 44).

When experimenting with diagonal cording anything is possible — leader cords can be selected at any point, and used in any direction. The effects which can be thus achieved are virtually limitless.

To work a simple zig-zag pattern in diagonal cording, set on 8 cords, each 48 in., on a

*Belt in a close pattern of diagonal cording.*

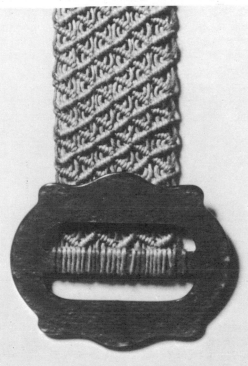

3 cords for the moment unworked. * *
**Next row:** leave first 5 cords unworked; tie 3 flat knots; leave final 5 cords unworked. * * *

Repeat from * to * * * three times, then repeat from * to * *
Go back to the first 3 cords, and using the cord on far left as knotting cord work vertical cording on the 2nd and 3rd cords to the depth of flat knot pattern already worked.
In a similar way work 2 rows of vertical cording with the last cord as knotting cord on right-hand side of flat knot pattern.
When vertical cording is complete at both sides, take the last cord round a pin at right-hand side of work, and use it as a leader to work a row of horizontal cording from right to left across all cords. At the end of the row reverse the direction of leader round a pin and work a second row of horizontal cording immediately belo
**TO FINISH.** Trim ends to give fringe of required depth.

*Cording can be used to draw shapes and figures — as in this knotted insert from a table runner.*

holding cord (16 working ends, each 24 in.). Attach a leader cord 30 in. long at top left-hand corner. Now position this at an angle across knotting cords, as shown in the diagram below, and secure it to working surface.

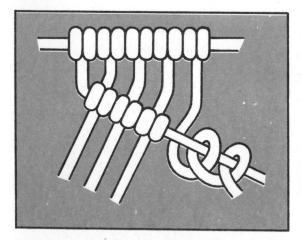

* Working from left to right, knot double half hitches with each vertical cord over the leader cord, making certain leader cord is kept absolutely taut.

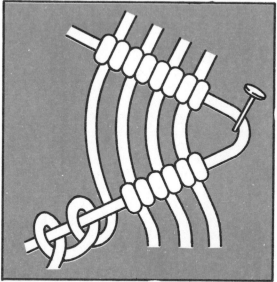

When you have worked across the row, insert a pin close to the last knot, bring leader cord round pin and take across work at the same angle as before, pinning it securely to working surface at opposite side. If your working surface is marked out in squares this will give you a useful set of guide lines for keeping diagonals uniform.

Work across row from right to left, working double half hitches over leader cord as before.** Repeat from * to ** until work is desired length. A similar zig-zag pattern can be worked on any number of cords, depending on depth of zig-zag required.

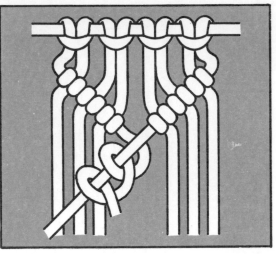

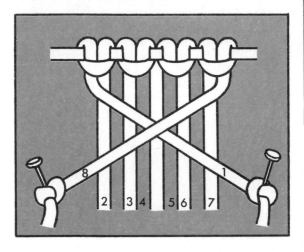

**Working a crossover.** Attractive crossover diagonals can be worked. Separate leaders may be attached at each side of work, or the 2 outer set-on cords can be used, as they are here. Cross them over and pin to the working surface.

When you reach the centre point the leader cords are linked, one cord becoming the knot-bearer, the other the knotting cord. It does not matter which one is used for which purpose, provided subsequent crossovers in the same design follow the same order. Our example shows the left-hand leader being knotted over the right-hand leader.

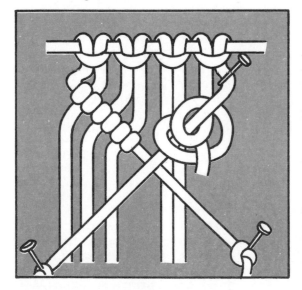

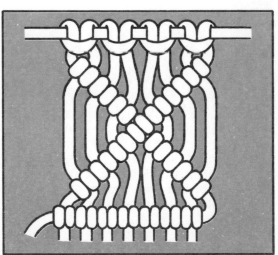

Now work double half hitches from left to right on the left diagonal leader cord, and from right to left on the right diagonal.

After the crossover the cording continues, working from the centre outwards.

45

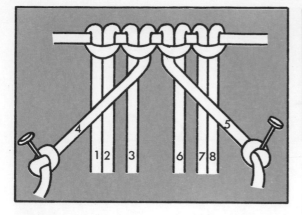

**Diamond patterns.** A diamond pattern may be created by starting from the centre point of your work. Take the 2 central vertical cords and place them diagonally across work one to each side, as shown above.

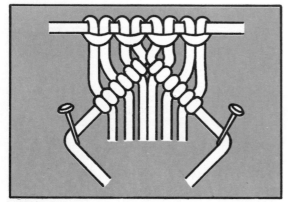

Work double half hitches over these cords, beginning in the centre and working outwards. When the row is completed, bring the leader cords back to the centre of work, as shown above, and knot another row of double half hitches over them.

A crossover may be formed at the end of this 2nd row with the leader cords, if wished, before continuing pattern, or the direction of each leader reversed round a pin, thus keeping the central points of the diamonds apart.

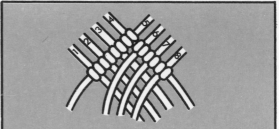

**Diamonds within diamonds.** In this pattern the 2 top edges of the diamond are worked first, knotting cords 4, 3, 2 and 1 over cord 5; and knotting cords 6, 7 and 8 over cord 4.

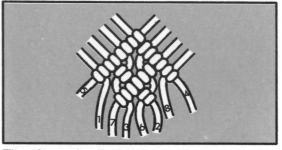

The 4 small diamonds in the centre are formed next: cord 3 is knotted over cord 2; cords 6, 2 and 3 are knotted over cord 7 (in that order); cord 6 is knotted over cord 2.

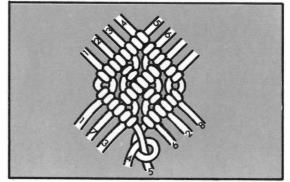

Finally the 2 remaining sides of the outer diamonds are formed by knotting cords 8, 2 and 6 over cord 4, and cords 1, 7, 3 and 4 over cord 5.

### Leaf patterns

A leaf pattern occurs frequently in traditional macramé designs. It can be used to considerable effect especially on bags and items where a fairly close patterning is required. This is merely a variation on diagonal cording. A leaf motif can be worked to any size to suit the item being made, but for practice

*Macramé band, English, early 20th century,
showing closely-worked leaf cording motifs.*

purposes it is best to work an 8-cord motif.
Cords therefore should be set on in multiples
of 8, plus 4 extra cords for the half motif
which will occur at the end of odd rows,
beginning of even rows. Allow a minimum
of 50 in. for each cut end.

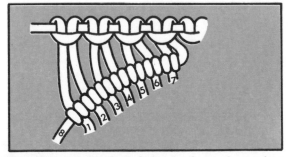

For the upper part of the leaf, cord number
8 is the leader, and cords 7, 6, 5, 4, 3, 2 and
1 are the knotting cords. Pin leader cord to
form top curve of leaf, and sloping down to
the left. Knot cords 7, 6, 5, 4, 3, 2 and 1 over
the leader in the order given.

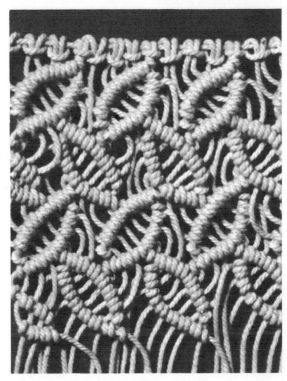

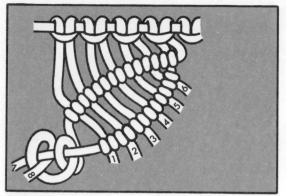

Now cord 7 becomes the leader. Pin it in a curve to form lower part of the same leaf, and knot cords 6, 5, 4, 3, 2, 1 and 8 over it. These 2 rows are worked across each group of 8 cords.

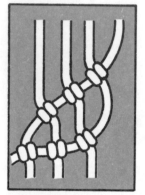

The 4 cords at the end are used to form a half motif. Cord 4 therefore becomes leader for the top curve of leaf but when you pin it in position begin the curve so it is level with the midway point of the top curve of the complete motif on the left. Now knot cords 3, 2 and 1 over it. For the lower curve of the leaf, cord 3 becomes leader, and cords 2, 1 and 4 are knotted over it.

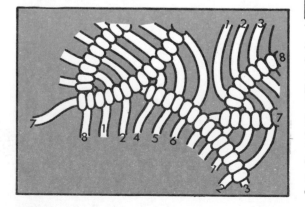

To work the top curve of the next row of leaves cord 3 becomes the leader for the first complete motif. Pin it in a curve as before but this time the curve should slope from left to right. Knot over it cords 4, 5 and 6 of the first motif, followed by 7, 8, 1 and 2 of the 2nd motif.

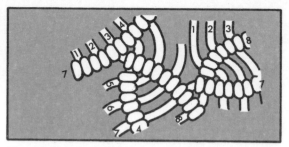

To complete lower curve of this leaf cord 4 is the leader, and cords 5 and 6 of the first motif are knotted over it, followed by cords 7, 8, 1 and 2 of the 2nd motif, and finally by cord 3 of the first motif. This sounds complicated but if you follow the diagrams carefully and work a practice sample yourself you will soon get the idea. This process also serves to show you how one cord can be made to travel to a totally different part of the pattern.

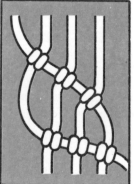

This second band of leaves is repeated across the work. The half motif this time will occur at the beginning of the row: cord 7 (from first motif of previous band) will become leader for the top curve of leaf. Begin the curve so it is level with the midway point of the top curve of the complete motif on the right (2nd band). Knot over it cords 8, 1 and 2 of the first motif of previous band. Cord 8 now becomes leader for bottom curve of leaf and cords 1, 2 and 7 are worked over it.

These 2 bands of leaf motifs form the pattern and are repeated throughout until work is desired length.

**Note.** When an alternating pattern such as this involves half motifs, the half motif should occur at the end of the row where all the cords can be knotted and still remain in position for the subsequent row. For instance, in this pattern, if the half motif had been positioned at the beginning of the first and subsequent odd numbered bands of the pattern, and at the end of the second and subsequent even numbered bands, instead of vice versa, then the leader cord for the upper part of the leaf would have been left 'floating' without any way of bringing it down to join the next row of motifs.

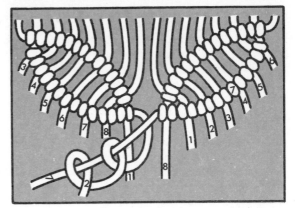

cords 1 and 16 are the leaders used to form top curve of leaves A and B. In the second row, cords 2 and 15 become leaders for lower curves of the same leaves.

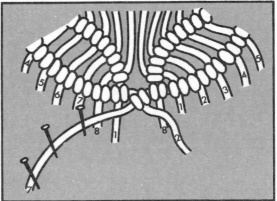

The leaders are then crossed by knotting cord 2 over cord 15, and cord 15 continues across work to become leader for the top curve of leaf C; cords 1, 8, 7, 6, 5, 4 and 3 are knotted over it.

**4-leaf motif.** This is a variation on the leaf pattern in which 4 motifs are linked together. Cords should be set on in multiples of 16 (no half motif is involved, so no extra 4 cords are required). In the first row,

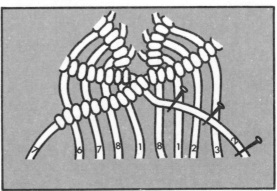

Cord 2 continues as leader for top curve of leaf D; cords 16, 9, 10, 11, 12, 13 and 14 are knotted over it.

Complete motif by knotting cords 8, 7, 6, 5, 4, 3 and 15 over 1, and cords 9, 10, 11, 12, 13, 14 and 2 over 16.

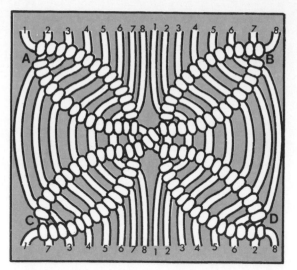

A few other variations on the leaf pattern can be seen in the examples shown throughout the book (see particularly the Victorian band shown on page 47). Leaf patterns can be worked close together to create a dense fabric, or with areas of unworked cords for an open-work effect. The leaf shape can have double outlines at top and bottom, or it can incorporate other knots in the centre of the leaf if wished.

### Two borders to make

Using horizontal and diagonal cording

### Border 1 (illustrated right)

**YARN.** Fine crochet cotton.
**MEASUREMENT.** Finished border measures 2 in. by $1\frac{1}{2}$ in.
**PREPARATION.** Cut 14 threads, each 18 in. Double them and set them with reversed double half hitches on to a holding cord, approximately 8 in. long. You now have 28 working ends.
**TO MAKE.** Pin a separate leader cord, about 18 in. long, to working surface at top left hand corner, and work a row of horizontal cording from left to right with all cords. Divide cords into groups of 4. Work on first group of 4 only: * take cord 1 as leader and slant it down to the right. Work diagonal cording over it with cords 2, 3 and 4.

Now work 2 more rows of diagonal cording immediately below, using the cord on the far left as leader for each row — i.e. cord 2 will be leader for second row, cord 3 leader for third. At the end of each row the leader drops down to become a knotting cord in the subsequent row.* *
Repeat from * to * * on each group of 4 cords across row.
Pin a separate leader, about 8 in. long, at left-hand side of work. Work a row of horizontal cording over it with all cords. Now repeat pattern of triple rows of diagonal cording, but reverse the direction of each set of rows — i.e. first 3 rows will slant down to the left, next 3 rows will slant down to the

50

right — and so on.
Attach a separate leader, about 8 in. long, to left-hand side of work, and work a row of horizontal cording over it with all cords.

**TO FINISH.** Trim ends to give required depth of fringe. Tie overhand knots in leader cords close to knotting, and trim ends close to overhand knots.

## Border 2 (illustrated bottom left)

**YARN.** Thick crochet cotton.

**MEASUREMENT.** Finished border measures 4 in. by 2½ in.

**PREPARATION.** Cut 16 threads, each 2 ft. long. Double them and set them with reversed double half hitches on to a holding cord approximately 10 in. long (32 working ends).

**TO MAKE.** Pin a separate leader cord, about 10 in. long, to working surface at top left-hand corner, and work a row of horizontal cording from left to right with all cords. Divide cords into groups of 8. Work on first group of 8 only: * take cord 8 as leader slanting down to the left, and work diagonal cording over it with cords 7, 6, 5, 4, 3, 2 and 1. Work a second row of diagonal cording immediately below with cord 7 as leader, and knotting over it cords 6, 5, 4, 3, 2, 1 and 8. * * Repeat from * to * * on each group of 8

cords across row.
Leave first 4 cords unworked then take next cord (cord 3 of first motif) and use it as leader slanting down to the right. Work diagonal cording over it with cords 4, 5 and 6 of first motif, then 7, 8, 1 and 2 of second motif.

Work a second row of diagonal cording immediately below the previous one, using cord 4 of first motif as leader and knotting over it cords 5 and 6 of first motif, and cords 7, 8, 1 and 2 of second motif, and finally cord 3 of first motif.

Repeat this motif across row twice more. Leave final 4 cords unworked.

Pin a separate leader cord, about 10 in. long, to left-hand side, and work a row of horizontal cording with all cords.

**TO FINISH.** Thread beads on to ends of leader cords. Trim fringe.

## Simple cording sampler

This sampler shows by contrast to the two previous borders how cording can be used to create an interesting open-weave effect. Where cords are left open in this way, careful pinning will produce regular curves.

**YARN.** Parcel string.

**MEASUREMENT.** Finished sampler measures approximately 10 in. by 3 in.

**PREPARATION.** Cut 6 threads each 8 ft. long. Double them and set them with reversed double half hitches on to a holding cord about 9 in. long (12 working ends).

**TO MAKE.** Take cord 1 as leader and slant it down to the right across work. Work diagonal cording over it with cords 2, 3, 4, 5 and 6. Similarly work a row of cording slanting down to the left over cord 12 with cords 11, 10, 9, 8 and 7.

Link the 2 leaders by knotting cord 12 over cord 1.

Work a second row of cording slanting down to the right immediately below the first with cord 2 as leader. Knot over it cords 3, 4, 5, 6 and 12.

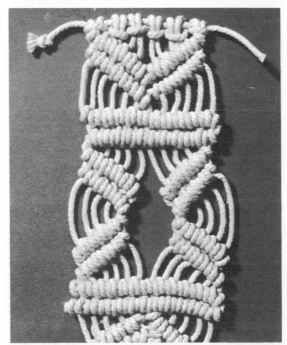

Similarly work a second row of diagonal cording slanting down to the left, using cord 11 as leader and knotting over it cords 10, 9, 8, 7 and 1.

Link these two leaders by knotting cord 11 over cord 2.

Cords now lie in the following order: 3, 4, 5, 6, 12, 11, 2, 1, 7, 8, 9 and 10.

With cord 3 as leader work a row of horizontal cording across all cords. At the end of the row, reverse direction of leader around a pin, and work a second row of horizontal cording from right to left.

Divide cords into 2 groups of 6. Work on first group of 6:

With cord 3 as leader slanting down to the right, work diagonal cording over it with cords 4, 5, 6, 12 and 11.

Work a second row of diagonal cording immediately below with cord 4 as leader, and knotting over it cords 5, 6, 12, 11 and 3.

Now reverse direction of cord 4 round a pin and work a row of diagonal cording slanting to the left with cords 3, 11, 12, 6 and 5.

Work a second row of diagonal cording im-mediately below with cord 3 as leader, and knotting over it cords 11, 12, 6, 5 and 4.

Repeat this pattern with other group of 6 cords, but have first 2 rows of cording slanting to the left (cords 10 and 9 as leaders), and then second 2 rows slanting to the right (cords 9 and 10 as leaders). Work 2 rows of horizontal cording with cord 3 as leader.

Working from centre out, take cord 2 as leader and work diagonal cording slanting to the left with cords 11, 12, 6, 5, 4 and 3. Now take cord 11 as leader slanting to the right and work diagonal cording over it with cords 1, 7, 8, 9 and 10.

Work a second row of cording slanting to the left with cord 1 as leader, and knotting over it cords 12, 6, 5, 4, 3 and 2.

Similarly, work a second row of cording slanting to the right with cord 12 as leader, and knotting over it cords 7, 8, 9, 10 and 11. Cords should now be back in their original and correct numerical order from 1 to 12.

**TO FINISH.** Trim ends to depth of fringe required.

## Sampler of mixed knots

Flat knots, half hitches, cording.

**PREPARATION.** Cut 23 threads, each 5 ft. long; cut one thread 7 ft. 6 in. Double the 23 threads and mount them with reversed double half hitches on to a holding cord approximately 9 in. long. Now set on the extra long thread on the left of the 23, but double it so the right-hand strand is the same length as other ends, and all the extra length is with cord 1. You should now have 48 working ends. Position threads on your working surface so the knot of the reversed double half hitches is face down (i.e. it will not be visible on right side of finished knotting).

**YARN.** The sampler illustrated is made in a medium-weight cotton twine. The finished work measures 5 in. by 6½ in., excluding fringe.

**TO MAKE. 1st row:** work horizontal cording from left to right with all cords, using cord 1 as leader. At end of row,

*Opposite: sculptured macramé head in ordinary parcel string. Cords were set on at centre of crown, and knotting moulded over a wig stand.*

Room divider worked in heavy rope, in different arrangements of the alternate flat knot pattern.

Hanging entitled 'Year In, Year Out' depicts the progression of the seasons from spring through to winter. Worked in rug wool, chenille, raffia, sisal and knitting wool, with a ring from an embroidery hoop and wooden beads incorporated in knotting pattern reverse direction of leader round pin.

**2nd row:** horizontal cording over leader. Divide cords into 12 groups of 4.

Work double chains of alternate half hitches: 6 knots from each side (12 half hitches altogether) on each group of 4 cords.

Using cord 1 again as the leader, work 1 row of horizontal cording.

**Next row:** work 4-end flat knots across row, tying each knot from right to left (i.e. begin first knotting sequence by taking right-hand cord under central core cords and over left-hand cord).

Now work on first 24 cords only.

* Leave first 2 cords unworked; tie 5 flat knots; leave last 2 cords unworked.

**Next row:** leave first 4 cords unworked; tie 4 flat knots; leave last 4 cords unworked.

**Next row:** leave first 6 cords unworked; tie 3 flat knots; leave last 6 cords unworked.

**Next row:** leave first 8 cords unworked; tie 2 flat knots; leave last 8 cords unworked.

**Next row:** leave first 10 cords unworked; tie 1 flat knot; leave last 10 cords unworked.

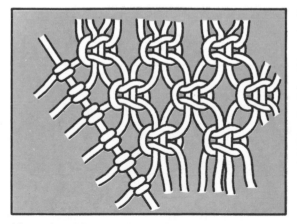

You should now have formed a triangular 'V' shape of flat knots. The cord at the top of the triangle at the far left now becomes a leader cord. Lay it down left-hand side of triangle close to the flat knots, and work diagonal cording over it from left to right with all the cords on that side.

Work another row of diagonal cording immediately below this first row, this time using the cord on the far left as leader. At the end of the row, the leader from previous row becomes a knotting cord and is worked over the new leader.

In a similar way, work a double row of diagonal cording down right-hand side of

triangle.

Link the leaders from either side by laying left-hand leader across right-hand leader, and working a double half hitch, using the right-hand leader as the knotting cord.

Leave these cords pinned in position while the curved chains are worked.

Work on first 11 cords only: work alternate half hitch chains with the first 3 cords, knotting cord 1 on its own, and 2 and 3 as a double thickness. Work 10 half hitches from each side (20 half hitches altogether).

The remaining 8 cords are divided into pairs and single alternate half hitch chains worked with each: 9 knots from each side for the first chain; 7 knots from each side for the 2nd chain; 5 knots from each side for the 3rd chain; 3 knots from each side for the 4th chain.

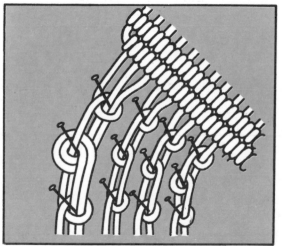

Curve these chains as shown in diagram, and pin them in position to the working surface.

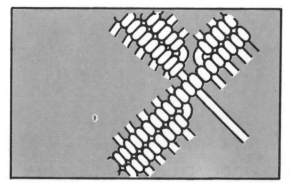

Now work a row of diagonal cording, from right to left, over leader which has crossed from right-hand part of motif, and continuing the same slope of the right-hand diagonal cording already worked. Work a 2nd row of diagonal cording immediately below, using cord on the far right as leader, and knotting leader from previous row over it at the end of the row.

Work on the 11 right-hand cords in a similar way, to form other side of motif. The 3-cord chain will be on the far right this time. And the first row of diagonal cording will be worked from left to right over leader from the left-hand side of motif, and will continue the slope of the left-hand diagonal cording already worked.

Working from the point of the triangle down, tie 1 flat knot, combining 2 ends from left-hand cording with 2 ends from right-hand cording. Work in the alternate flat knot pattern, bringing in an extra pair of cords from each side on every row until you have worked the row with 5 flat knots in it.**

Repeat from * to ** for remaining 24 cords.

**Next row:** work flat knots across all cords. Cord on far right now becomes leader. Work a row of horizontal cording from right to left over this leader. At the end of the row reverse direction of leader around a pin and work a 2nd row of horizontal cording immediately below the first.

**TO FINISH.** Trim ends evenly to form fringe approximately 2 in. deep.

## WORKING WITH MULTIPLE STRANDS

So far we have worked with one strand of yarn at a time — be it thick or thin — and certainly while still in the experimental stages it is as well to continue with a single thickness, for knots are simpler to manipulate, and it is easier to keep cords flat and in order.

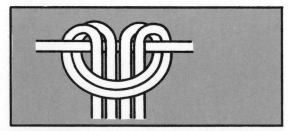

However very interesting effects can be obtained by working the various knots and techniques so far described in double or even treble thicknesses of yarn. For instance,

try working border 1 shown on page 50 using double thicknesses of rug wool instead of a single thickness of crochet cotton. This means you will cut 28 ends of wool (instead of 14 as for single-thickness border). The cords will be mounted in the same way but in pairs as shown in diagram, below. From then on, each double thickness is treated as a single cord.

You will probably find the knots take fractionally longer to tie because you must take care to keep the cords even and not twisted.

This example alone should demonstrate dramatically how by altering not only the yarn used, but its thickness you can achieve vastly different results. Further demonstrations of this can be seen on page 112.

# Sinnets and braids

A **sinnet** is an expression you will frequently come across not only in macramé work but in nautical terminology too – for this is where the term originated. It means simply a single chain of knots, as opposed to a fabric composed of multiples of knots and pattern motifs.

A sinnet may consist of any of the knots so far explained. Some of these have distinctive names of their own. A Solomon's bar, for instance, is a sinnet of Solomon's – or flat – knots. All the variations on the half hitch, as shown on pages 32 and 33, when worked in chains are termed sinnets.

## Solomon's bar with picots

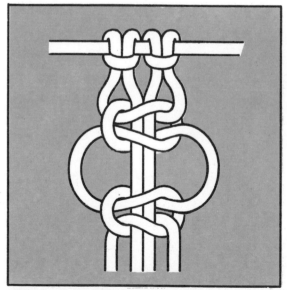

This is a variation on the flat knot sinnet which is simple to work and effective when used as a decorative edging. Work one flat knot then work a 2nd flat knot a little way down central core cords. Tighten the knot

then push it up into position below the first knot. This will create picots – or loops – at either side. Continue in this way.

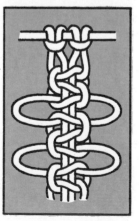

The sinnet can be varied by working picots only between alternate pairs of knots, or between every 3rd and 4th knot. It can also

be worked on triple knots: work a flat knot followed by a half knot (i.e. a triple knot), then a little way down central core cords work another triple knot. Tighten and push 2nd triple knot up close to the first, thus forming picots at either side of work. Continue in this way to form sinnet.

## Cording braids

Cording in any of its many variations can be used to form sinnets too, and these make attractive braids with which to trim a dress, jumper or blouse, or any household article — a plain lampshade or cushion cover, for instance. Alternatively braids can be used on their own as hairbands, chokers, bracelets, shoe straps. In fact any of the samplers shown here as well as providing a valuable exercise in knotting techniques can also serve a decorative and useful purpose as well (see also note on samplers, page 136).

The handle of the Italian Cavandoli bag, pictured on page 17, is worked on a cording braid principle.

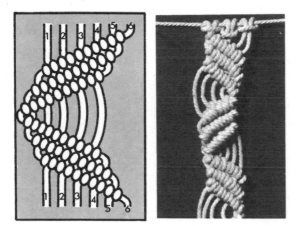

Braid worked on 6 cords with diagonal cording, 3 rows of diagonal cording sloping to the right alternated with 3 rows of diagonal cording sloping to the left. Begin with 3 rows sloping to the right. Cord 1 is used as the leader for the first row, cord 2 for the 2nd row, cord 3 for the 3rd row.
Cords now lie in the following order, from left to right: 4, 5, 6, 1, 2, 3. Cord 3 becomes the leader for the first row of cording sloping down to the left. In the next row cord 2 is

*Opposite: choker and belt made from simple alternate flat knot patterned braids.*

the leader, and in the next cord 1. Cords are now back in their original order. Continue in this way to length required.

Another cording braid this time with a separate leader attached at the top left-hand corner and held horizontally across work. At the end of each row, reverse direction of leader round pin and continue working horizontal cording, keeping each row of knots close to the previous one.

*Below: sampler of flat knot and half hitch sinnets and, far right, diagonal cording braids.*

Diagonal cording worked in the same direction throughout. Work it on as many cords as you wish, depending on the width required of finished braid — worked on only a few cords the braid makes a pretty hairband; on a greater number of cords it can be used as a sturdy bag handle. Work from left to right using the outside left-hand cord as leader for every row (see sampler on page 59, 2 right-hand chains).

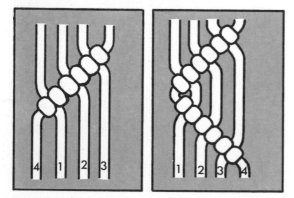

Braid worked on 8 cords with diagonal cording. Work first section of pattern on left-hand side only: working from centre out, use cord 4 as leader and knot cords 3, 2 and 1 over it in that order to form a diagonal sloping down to the left.

Cord 4 continues as leader and cords 1, 2 and 3 are knotted over it to form diagonal sloping down to the right.

Now work another row of cording immediately below with cord 1 as leader, and cords 2, 3 and 4 knotted over it.

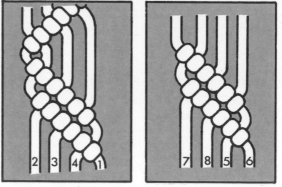

Work right-hand section: working from centre out, use cord 5 for leader and knot cords 6, 7 and 8 over it to form diagonal sloping down to the right.

Work another row of cording immediately below, with cord 6 as leader, and cords 7, 8 and 5 knotted over it.

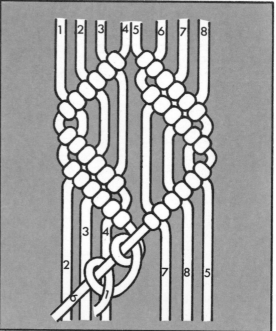

Cord 6 continues as leader for long diagonal sloping to the left. Work over it with cords 5, 8 and 7. Now link with left-hand part of pattern by knotting cords 1, 4, 3 and 2 over it. Continue in this way.

Work one half hitch as usual, then reverse the knot for the next loop, i.e. take knotting cord *under* knot-bearing cord and bring it up and over it to form loop. Draw knot tight. Continue in this way working a half hitch and a reversed half hitch alternately.

Another interesting braid using horizontal and diagonal cording. This could make an attractive belt. Work on as many cords as wished (our sampler shows 6). The outside left-hand cord is always used as leader for the horizontal cording, the outside right-hand cord for every diagonal row.

### Tatted bar braids

A simple variation on the half hitch, known as the **reversed double half hitch** (or tatting knot) is shown here. This is the knot you use to set on threads but when it is incorporated in a knotting pattern — as now — it is laid on its side. It can be worked from the left or the right.

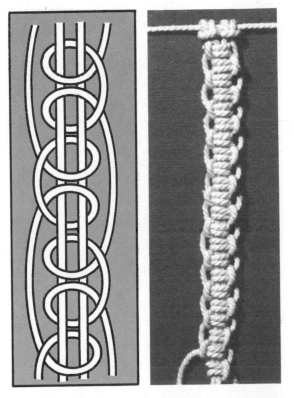

A braid formed from reversed double half hitches worked over a centre core — known as a **tatted bar** — again is excellent for bag handles and if made in a suitable yarn extremely strong. Here it is worked with 4 cords: 2 outer knotting cords, 2 central knot-bearing core cords. Work reversed double half hitches alternately from left and right. This braid can be worked with picots as for Solomon's bar with picots, merely by spacing the knots as required, then pushing them up to form loops of yarn at the sides.

**Variations on the tatted bar**

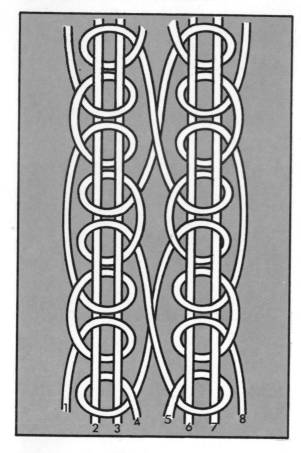

Work on 4 cords: 2 groups of reversed double half hitches are knotted alternately from left and right with outer cords over central core cords.

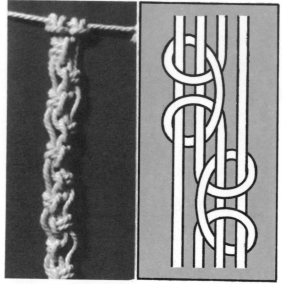

Work on 8 cords: reversed double half hitches are worked with 2 outside cords over cords 2 and 3, and 6 and 7 respectively. Then cord 5 knots a reversed double half hitch over cords 2 and 3, and cord 4 is crossed over cord 5 and knots a reversed double half hitch over cords 6 and 7.

Reversed double half hitches are worked with outside cords as in first row, then cord 4 is knotted over cords 2 and 3, and cord 5 is crossed over cord 4 and knotted over cords 6 and 7. Continue in this way, continually crossing cords 4 and 5. This gives a strong wide braid.

Work on 4 cords: the 2 central cords are used sometimes to knot, sometimes as knot-bearers. The 2 outer cords are knot-bearers all the time. Work a reversed double half hitch with cord 3 over cords 2 and 1, then work a reversed double half hitch with cord 2 over cords 3 and 4. Continue in this way.

## SAMPLER WALL HANGING

You have now learned all the basic knots and techniques of macramé. There are other knots and variations which are useful to know, and these follow in the subsequent chapters, but in fact if you stopped now you would still know enough macramé to be able to make a multitude of items, both useful and decorative.

The following sampler uses a variety of the basic knots and techniques. Instructions are given in full to take you through each section of the design, and when you have completed it you should be able to tell how almost any item shown in this book has been made, merely by studying the knot formation.

If you set on the threads for the sampler on a wooden rod the finished piece will make a most attractive wall hanging.

**YARN.** Heavy-weight cotton fishing line.
**MEASUREMENT.** Finished sampler measures approximately 16 in. long, 3½ in. wide, excluding fringe.
**TENSION CHECK.** Sinnet of 4 flat knots measures 1 in.
**PREPARATION.** Cut 12 threads, 11 at 4 yd., 1 at 6 yd. Double them and set them with reversed double half hitches on to a holding cord about 9 in. long, placing extra long end at far left, and setting on cord so the second working length end is the same length as all the others, and the entire area of extra length is in the first working end. You now have 24 working ends.
**TO MAKE. Pattern section 1.** Using cord on far left as leader, work a row of horizontal cording right across row with every cord. At the end of the row, reverse direction of leader round a pin and work a second row of horizontal cording immediately below the first.

Now divide cords into groups of 4 cords each and work flat knot sinnets with each group — work 6 knots in each sinnet.
**Divider 1:** using cord 1 again as leader work a row of horizontal cording right across on all cords, being sure to keep sinnets straight and the distance between each regular. Careful pinning will help. At the end of the row of cording, reverse the direction of leader round a pin, and work a second row of horizontal cording immediately below.
**Pattern section 2.** Divide cords into three groups of 8.

Working on first group of 8, cords numbered 1–8 for ease of identification: use cord 4 as leader slanting down to the left.
Work diagonal cording over it with cords 3, 2 and 1 in turn.
Similarly use cord 5 as leader slanting down to the right and work diagonal cording over it with cords 6, 7 and 8.
Tie a flat knot in centre using cords 1 and 8 as knotting cords, and tying knot over

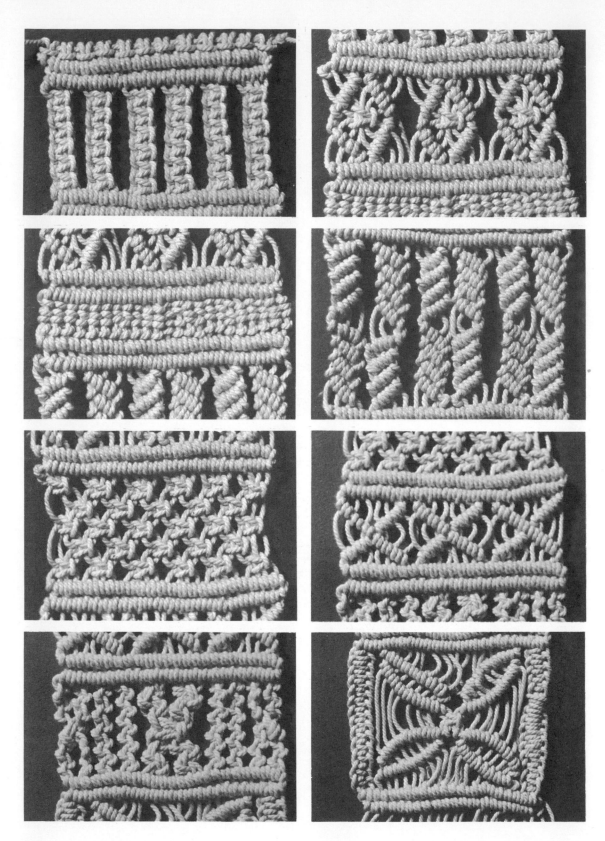

central knot-bearing core of cords 2, 3, 6 and 7.

Now bring cord 4 round a pin at side edge and let it continue as leader slanting down to the right. Work diagonal cording over it with cords 1, 2 and 3.

Similarly bring cord 5 round a pin, and slant it down to the left. Work diagonal cording over it with cords 8, 7 and 6. Again careful pinning will keep the diagonals even.

Repeat this knotting sequence with each of the other two groups of 8 cords.

**Divider 2:** as divider 1.

**Pattern section 3.** Work 2 rows of close vertical cording, using cord 1 as knotting cord throughout.

Work first row from left to right.

Reverse direction of cord 1 round a pin at the end of row, and work a second row from right to left.

**Divider 3:** as divider 1.

You may need to add a new leader in this divider, as the vertical cording will have used up cord 1 fairly quickly. Introduce the new leader from the wrong side of work, and leaving a few inches of cord at the back. Afterwards tie the end of the old cord to the new cord with a weaver's knot (see page 116).

**Pattern section 4.** * Take cord 4 as leader slanting down to the left, and work diagonal cording from right to left over it with cords 3, 2 and 1 in turn.

Now take cord 3 as leader slanting to the left and work a row of diagonal cording immediately below the previous one with cords 2, 1 and 4. Work 2 more rows of diagonal cording in a similar way, each row immediately below the previous one, and using the cord on the far right as leader for each row.

Cord 1 will therefore be leader for the 4th row. At the end of the row reverse the direction of cord 1 round a pin and let it become leader slanting down to the right. Work diagonal cording over it from left to right with cords 2, 3 and 4.

Work another 3 rows of diagonal cording slanting down to the right immediately below this one, using cord on far left as leader for each row.

*Opposite, left to right, top to bottom: close-up of pattern sections 1, 2, 3, 4, 5, 6, 7 and 8 of the sampler wall hanging.*

Now work on second group of 4 cords. Work as for first group, but reverse the direction of cording – i.e. first 4 rows will slant to the right. Second 4 rows will slant to the left.**

Repeat from * to ** for the third and fourth groups of 4 cords, and for the fifth and sixth groups.

**Divider 4:** as divider 1.

**Pattern section 5. 1st row:** work flat knots across all cords.

**2nd row:** leave first 2 cords unworked; work 5 flat knots; leave final 2 cords unworked.

Repeat first and 2nd rows once, then work first row again.

**Divider 5:** as divider 1.

**Pattern section 6.** Divide cords into 3 groups of 8. Work on first group of 8: Take cord 1 as leader and slant down to the right. Work diagonal cording over it with cords 2, 3 and 4.

Take cord 8 as leader, and slant down to the left. Work diagonal cording over it with cords 7, 6 and 5.

Link leaders by knotting cord 8 over cord 1. Let cord 1 continue at same slant across work and knot over it cords 5, 6 and 7. Let cord 8 continue as leader slanting to the left at other side, and knot over it cords 4, 3 and 2. Repeat this pattern motif with other two groups of 8.

**Divider 6:** as divider 1, except leader cord will now be cord 3, as it is positioned at far left of work.

**Pattern section 7.** Cords are now renumbered from 1–16 in the order in which they lie.

Work 4 alternate half hitches with cords 1 and 2 (i.e. 2 knots from each side). Work 4 alternate half hitches with cords 3 and 4. Link these 2 chains by working 2 double alternate half hitches with cords 1 and 2, and 3 and 4. Work 4 single alternate half hitches with cords 1 and 2. Work 4 single alternate half hitches with cords 3 and 4. With cords 5 and 6 work a single chain of alternate half hitches: 10 knots altogether (5 from each side).

Work a similar chain with cords 7 and 8. Now work a double alternate half hitch chain with cords 9 and 10, and 11 and 12: 3 knots altogether.

Work a similar chain with cords 13 and 14, and 15 and 16.

Link the 2 chains by tying a flat knot: use the 2 outer pairs of cords (9 and 10, and 15 and 16) as knotting cords; the remaining cords (11, 12, 13 and 14) as the central knot-bearing core.

Work a double alternate half hitch chain with cords 9 and 10, and 11 and 12: 3 knots altogether.

Work a similar chain with cords 13 and 14, and 15 and 16.

Work a single alternate half hitch chain with cords 17 and 18: 10 knots altogether.

Work a similar chain with cords 19 and 20. Work cords 21, 22, 23 and 24 as for cords 1, 2, 3 and 4.

**Divider 7:** as divider 1.

**Pattern section 8.** Using cord 4 as leader work top curve of a leaf motif slanting down to the right with cords 5, 6, 7, 8, 9, 10, 11 and 12.

Use cord 5 as leader for lower curve of leaf and knot over it cords 6, 7, 8, 9, 10, 11, 12 and 4.

Work a similar leaf motif but slanting in opposite direction with the next 9 cords –

i.e. cord 21 will be leader for top curve of leaf; cord 20 will be leader for lower curve of leaf.

Link these 2 leaves by tying a flat knot using cords 4 and 21 as knotting cords, and cords 5 and 20 as knot-bearing core.

Now let cord 5 form top curve of leaf motif slanting down to the left, and knot over it cords 4, 12, 11, 10, 9, 8, 7 and 6.

Use cord 4 as leader for lower curve of leaf and knot over it cords 12, 11, 10, 9, 8, 7, 6 and 5.

Work a similar leaf slanting in opposite direction at other side, so cord 20 forms leader for top curve of leaf; cord 21 is leader for lower curve.

Now work a Genoese bar with cords 1, 2 and 3 – i.e. knot alternate half hitches over cord 2 with cords 1 and 3. Work bar to depth of central leaf pattern.

Work a similar Genoese bar with cords 22, 23 and 24.

**Divider 8:** as divider 1.

**TO FINISH.** Trim fringe evenly to depth required.

*Modern macramé hanging worked in heavy string. Cording diamonds containing flat knots are separated by buttonhole bars.*

# Some fancy knots

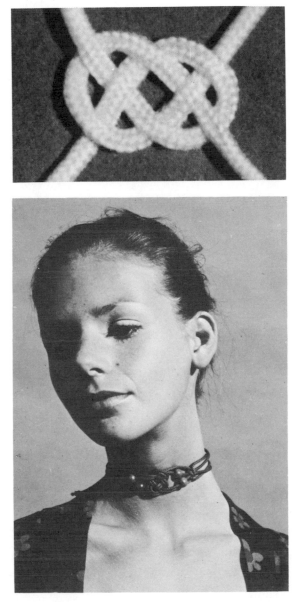

## JOSEPHINE KNOT

This is a decorative knot with a pleasing symmetrical appearance. Although complex looking, once mastered it is extremely simple to tie. It is best worked in thick rope-like yarns, or with multiple strands of finer yarns, and is a very useful knot for belts — see, for example, the two belts shown on page 141.

One is made in a very thick synthetic marine rope, and consists of just four equally spaced Josephine knots. It takes only moments to make and looks marvellous!

The other belt, made from a medium-weight fishing line, consists of a closely-worked sinnet of Josephine knots, alternating the direction of the knot each time to give a consistent line through the sinnet.

The Josephine knot, which is also known as the Chinese knot or Carrick bend, is worked with two or two groups of threads. Both cords are used for knotting, so there are no knot-bearers.

An attractive braid to use as a dress trimming can also be made from Josephine knots. It is also excellent for jewellery — see picture left, also bracelets on page 71.

Practise the knot with a fairly thick but flexible yard. Cut length of yarn to measure at least 1 yard. Double it and either set it on to a short holding cord, or pin it directly to your working surface through the loop. Alternatively, cut 2 separate strands, each 18 in., and pin them side by side to your working surface.

*Choker made from heavy cord, with a Josephine knot as the central motif.*

To work the knot from right to left, take right-hand cord and curve it up and under itself to form a big loop.

Hold this loop flat on working surface, or pin it to keep it in position, then bring left-hand cord down over loop, under lower section of right-hand cord, up and over top section of right-hand cord, then under top half of loop, over left-hand cord lying across loop, and under lower half of loop. Pull knot gently into position. It may be pulled tightly or left loose as wished.

To work a Josephine knot from left to right, merely make first loop with left-hand cord, then bring right-hand cord down over loop and weave it under, over, under, over and under as before.

Once you have got the idea, try tying the knot with double cords — you will instantly achieve a much more dramatic looking knot. Take care when working with multiple thicknesses of yarn always to keep the cords flat and in order or the knot will be irregular and will not lie flat. The easiest method to do this is to work the knot without worrying unduly about the order of the cords and then pull it halfway into shape. At this stage using a pin or a fine knitting needle, adjust the cords into their right order. Finally pull the knot as tightly as wished.

### JAPANESE KNOT

The Japanese knot is an even more elaborate knot than the Josephine and impressive in very decorative work especially when used to form a central motif of a pattern. It is based on flat knots and probably owes its name and origin to the Japanese people's predilection for tying up their gift parcels with complex and beautiful arrangements of knots. Wire and cord are often knotted together and after the knots have been worked the wires are bent into various decorative shapes: leaves, flowers and geometric forms.

been flat or two-dimensional. There are however various other knots which are three-dimensional or — as I tend to think of them — 'solid'. These solid knots have a variety of uses: they add interesting surface texture to a pattern, or they can serve a functional purpose by collecting several ends together. They can even be used to disguise an awkward join or a mistake in your work!

### Bead knot

Also known as a pearl knot, or a flat knot ball, this knot is effective in the centre of a diamond pattern or in any design which is focused to a central point.

Work with a minimum of 4 ends, each approximately 2 ft. long. Tie a flat knot with outer cords over central cords. Then form each outer cord into a curve, as in diagram, above. Pin to working surface to keep in place, if necessary.

Loop left-hand inner cord round left-hand outer cord, taking it over, up and under. Loop right-hand inner cord round right-hand outer cord, taking it under, up and over.

Bring the inner cords back to centre of work and tie a flat knot with them (there will of course be no central knot-bearing cords in this case).

Now take left-hand inner cord out to loop round left-hand outer cord, this time looping it under, up and over. Loop right-hand inner cord round right-hand outer cord, looping it over, up and under. Complete the Japanese knot with a flat knot, knotting outer cords over central inner cords.

### THE 'SOLID' KNOTS

So far most of the knots you have met have

*The bead knot can form a focal point in the centre of a motif.*

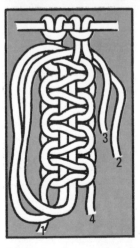

Make a sinnet of 4 flat knots, then take the central knot-bearing cords up and pass them back over the top of the sinnet, above the first knot and between the 2 pairs of cords.

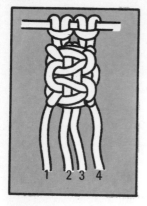

Pull the cords down on the wrong side of work, being sure to keep them in their correct order. The sinnet will form itself into a ball or bead effect on the front of work. Work another flat knot with the outer cords over the central ones to hold the bead in place. If you want a larger, chunkier bead, work a longer sinnet of flat knots before taking central cords up and over. For a small bead, work a sinnet of 3 flat knots only (this is the minimum number that can be worked to achieve a satisfactory bead knot).

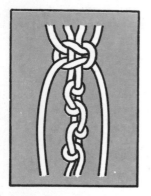

A similar effect can be achieved by working first a flat knot on all 4 cords, then a chain of alternate half hitches on the central 2 cords only — a minimum of 4 half hitches will be required (2 from each side), but again more can be worked for a bigger bead.

Take central cords up and over to the back of work, as for the flat knot bead, and complete by tying a flat knot over central cords with outer cords. This form of bead is slightly neater and rounder than the flat knot bead.

## Shell knot

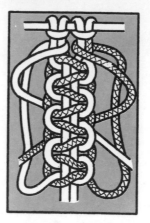

This is another variation of the bead knot. Begin as for the flat knot bead with a sinnet of 4 flat knots, then take the outer cords up behind the sinnet and through to the front of work above first knot in sinnet.

Bring left-hand cord down over left-hand pair of cords at the top, and right-hand cord down over right-hand pair. Take both cords to the back of work again, cross them over and bring them back to the front through the loops formed at the sides of sinnet. Complete with a tightly tied flat knot.

## Overhand knot

The overhand knot which you have been using to anchor holding cords to the working surface can also be used to create interesting pattern effects both on its own and combined with other knots. Other versions of its name are thumb knot and round knot.

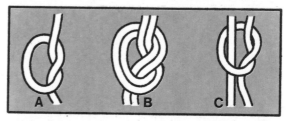

The overhand is one of the few knots which can be worked on one cord only (diagram A).

*Opposite, left: poncho and bag in heavy cord, mainly flat knots. Top right: choker with centre front fastening, in Josephine and flat knots. Bottom right: Josephine knot bracelet with beads.*

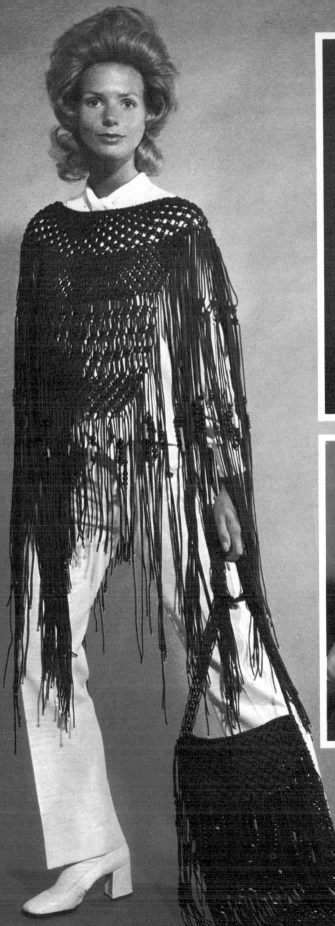
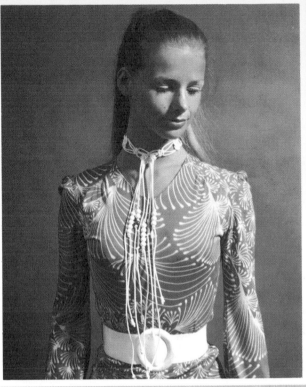

It can, if wished, be worked on 2 — or more — cords together (diagram B), or it can be worked on a single cord over a knot-bearing cord (diagram C). At the end of your work, if you tie each cord individually with an overhand knot this will prevent the cords fraying. It is also useful as you see in a later chapter for holding beads and other forms of decoration in place.

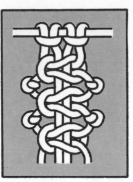

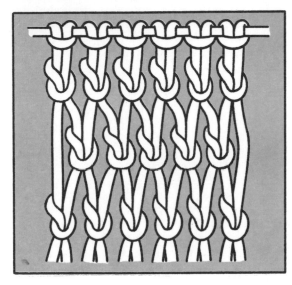

A pattern similar to the alternate flat knot pattern can be worked with overhand knots. Work across first row tying cords together in pairs with overhand knots — the left-hand cord in every case will be the knotting cords, the right-hand cords the knot-bearers. In the 2nd row, leave first cord unworked, then knot 2nd cord over 3rd cord, and so on across the row. Leave last cord unworked. The 3rd row will be the same as the first, and the 4th the same as 2nd. Continue in this way.

### Variations on the overhand knot

Two overhand knots tied in the same double cords close together, one tied from right to left, the other tied from left to right, create an interesting geometric shaped knot.

*Opposite, top: bag in multi-coloured rug wools worked in a free knotting pattern. The bag is lined and has a plaited handle.*
*Below: chess set made in dyed parcel string. Basic pattern is alternate flat knots, but flat knot loops are used to indicate relative importance of each piece in the game.*

Solomon's bar with picots of overhand knots: work a flat knot, then work overhand knots in each of the 2 outer cords, followed by another flat knot. Continue in this way pushing each knot close to the previous one. This makes a good decorative braid, attractive for shoulder straps or any sort of dress trimming. The overhand knot picots may be spaced out if wished, only worked between alternate flat knots, or between every 3rd and 4th flat knot.

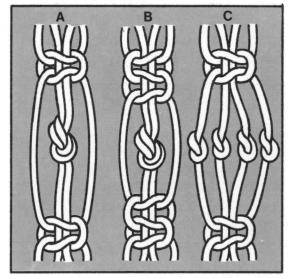

Three other ways to combine flat and over-hand knots: work a Solomon's bar but tie an overhand knot between each pair of flat knots with the central core cords (diagram A); in diagram B triple knots are alternated with overhand knots tied in the central core cords; in diagram C separate overhand knots are tied in each of the 4 cords, between each pair of flat knots.

**The true lover's knot.** There are several versions of this romantically named sailor's knot, but each is based on the intertwining of 2 overhand knots.

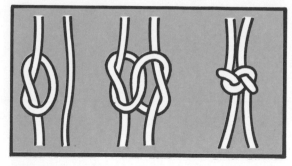

Work with 2 cords: tie an overhand knot in the left-hand cord by taking the cord up and under itself, from right to left, then down through the loop formed.

Leave the knot loose, then work an overhand knot in the right-hand cord, passing it under the loop of the left-hand knot, then up and over itself, from left to right, then down through the loop formed.

Pull both knots gently closed, easing them so they are even and regular. The knot should be perfectly symmetrical and give the appearance of a single knot.

It is the exquisite uniformity of this knot which has given it its romantic name. Many years

ago it was customary for sailors to give their sweethearts two rings of gold wires linked by a true lover's knot. The twin rings could move independently but once linked by this knot they could not be separated: such a symbolic gift was no doubt reassuring to the young couple when kept apart by a long sea voyage.

Jewellers often attempted to copy the knotting device in their gold rings but by using a single wire instead of two, they failed to reproduce the knot accurately and the twin rings were rigid and unable to move independently.

True lover's knots worked closely together can produce a pattern similar to — yet quite different from — solid cording. The magnificent Moroccan border on page 35 is worked throughout in true lover's knots. The solid 'background' is created from closely worked true lover's knots; the decorative motifs on each panel are formed from different arrangements of true lover's knots, sometimes worked in double or multiple cords, and combined with rows of diagonal cording.

A close-up of one section of the border is shown below. Although there are 48 panels in this border, and only true lover's knots and cording are used, every single panel has a different pattern from the others.

*Each of the 42 panels of this Moroccan border is a different arrangement of true lover's knots.*

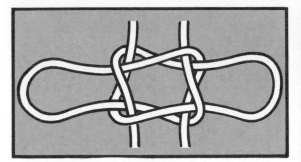

An interesting and attractive variation on the true lover's knot can be worked by taking hold of the 2 central intertwined loops and pulling each in the direction it is facing out between the outer cords to form picots at the sides. A crochet hook is useful here for catching hold of the loops.

A false lover's knot is simply a true lover's knot worked in reverse, i.e. left-hand overhand knot is worked by taking cord up and over itself. The right-hand cord is linked to the left-hand cord loop as before then taken under itself. If the central loops are taken out to form picots as described above, and the knot worked in a strong cord, this can be used as a decorative frogging fastening.

## Chinese crown knot

In appearance this knot is similar to the true lover's knot but in fact it is worked in a totally different way. It is essential you work on a soft board or surface suitable for pinning — an ironing board is ideal. Work with two cords (or two double thicknesses).

Coil left-hand cord as shown in diagram A, pinning it in place as you work. Now take right-hand cord and weave it in and out of the bends of the left-hand cord, as shown in diagram B.
**Note.** The weaving is not regular — it is under 1 cord, over 2 cords, under 3 cords, over 2 and under 1. Pull knot into position.

*Top to bottom: true lover's knot with picots; false lover's knot with picots; Chinese crown.*

## Turk's head

This is a simplified form of a complex series of sailor's knots generally worked over cylindrical objects, but also tied in heavy rope to use as fenders on the boats. The knot is worked from a single cord looped round on itself many times, and can be worked flat or formed into a three-dimensional ball as required.

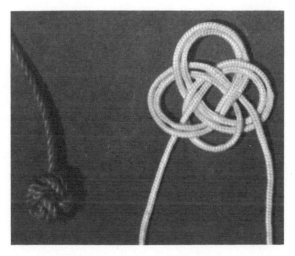

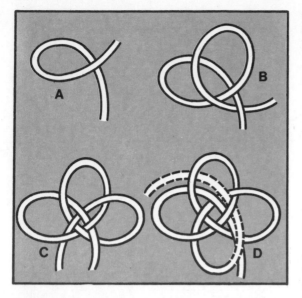

Begin by forming a loop as in diagram A. Form a 2nd loop, overlapping the first, and take cord end behind cord leading down to the first loop (diagram B). Form a 3rd overlapping loop, this time weaving the cord over, under, over and under other loops as you come to them (diagram C). Take cord over cord leading down to first loop, then weave it under, over and under cords of 3rd and 2nd loops (diagram D).

Now repeat the whole process, taking cord on the same course as before for first, 2nd and 3rd loops, being careful to weave cord over and under other loops at exactly the same place as before. Make sure all the cords lie in order and flatten out knot evenly.

If it is wished to convert the knot into a solid ball, gradually ease the various loops of cord until the knot forms itself into a rounded ball shape. If preferred, the knot can be eased to form a cylindrical shape. This knot is effective at the end of cords or on belt ends or it can be used to form buttons.

## Monkey's fist

This knot has a similar appearance to the Turk's head, but it is nearly always worked over a bead, marble, glass ball or other suitable hard object to give it solidity (see Moroccan panel, page 35).

Sailors give weight to heaving lines by working a monkey's fist at the end of the line over a heavy iron or lead ball. Used in macramé work, it can serve a similar purpose by giving weight to the end of a cord. An attractive pendant · necklace, for instance, can be made by working a narrow flat braid, joining it into a circle, and adding a monkey's fist tied over a heavy marble or bead, or even pebble, at the centre front.

The monkey's fist is tied with a single cord (or double thickness of cord). There are many ways of working the knot, but every method is based on winding the yarn round on itself, as you would wind a ball of wool or string. Traditionally sailors wound the knot on their hand and this is the method described here. Begin at the point where you want the knot to be positioned and making sure you have a good length of cord remaining, wind cord vertically round three fingers of one hand three times (winding towards end of cord). Keep your middle and third fingers slightly apart as you wind.

Stop third wind opposite gap in your fingers, take cord to the back and make three horizontal windings from left to right, round the vertical cords. Bring cord down through middle of horizontal windings then through to the front of work.

At this point carefully take cord off your hand and insert a suitable sized marble or bead into the centre of the wound cord. Make three more vertical windings over the central horizontal windings (within the first vertical windings) to enclose the bead or marble. To close outside windings into a ball shape gently pull each winding of the cord to tighten it until the ball is regular.

The end of the cord can either be cut and tucked back into the ball to conceal cut end, or else taken up and attached to cord where it comes from the rest of work with a double half hitch, overhand knot or reversed double half hitch whichever is most consistent with the knotting pattern.

The monkey's fist is a somewhat fiddly knot to work, for pulling the loose windings into shape needs patient concentration. Your first efforts will probably not be a hundred per cent successful – the windings may become uneven, the bead fall out! And the knot will most likely end up far from the point at which you'd intended it. Persevere however – for once you've got the knack the knot will fall nicely into shape, and the finished result is well worth the initial effort!

## Coil knot

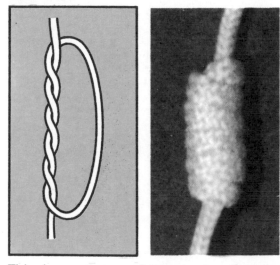

This is another useful knot for finishing ends but can also be worked to form part of a pattern. Form a large loop at the point where you wish coil to appear. At the point where the loop crosses, wind cord several times round itself (the number of winds determines the depth of finished coil). Gently pull both ends of the cord and the winds will form themselves into a coil.

## Berry knot

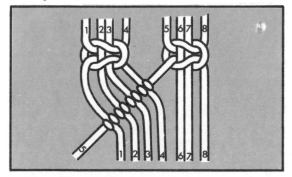

Also called bell knot, there are various methods of working this interesting textured knot. The simplest is as follows: work with a minimum of 8 cords (or multiples thereof).

Tie a flat knot in the first group of 4, and a flat knot in the 2nd group, then using cord 5 as a leader work diagonal cording sloping down to the left with cords 4, 3, 2 and 1.

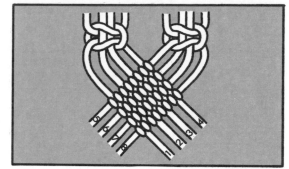

Now cord 6 becomes the leader, and cords 4, 3, 2 and 1 are knotted over it, immediately below the first row of cording. The 3rd row is worked with cord 7 as leader, followed by a row with cord 8 as leader. Start each row close to the 2nd flat knot – the cording motif will gradually pull over to the right.

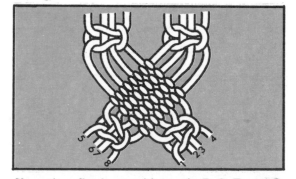

Now tie a flat knot with cords 5, 6, 7 and 8. As you tie the first half of the flat knot

gently push your fingers inside the 'berry' pushing it out to form a rounded shape at the front of work. Complete flat knot and tie another on the opposite side of berry with cords 1, 2, 3 and 4.

Try working the berry knot in an alternate pattern with open areas of unworked cords between, or combine a few berry knots with a braid to make an attractive necklace. If wished, the berries can be stuffed with cotton wool to give a slightly more substantial berry.

### Solid knot sampler

**YARN.** Thick gold yarn.
**MEASUREMENT.** Finished sampler measures approximately 6 in. square.
**PREPARATION.** Cut 12 threads each 4 ft. long. Double them and set them with reversed double half hitches on to a holding cord about 12 in. long (24 working ends).
**TO MAKE.** Each pattern motif is worked on 12 cords, so divide cords into two groups of 12 each. Now work on the first group only (cords numbered from 1–12 for ease of identification):
\* Tie 3 overhand knots with cords 1 and 2, tying the knots with both cords together, and reversing the direction of the 2nd knot (i.e. begin first knot from right to left, begin 2nd knot from left to right, begin 3rd knot from right to left).
Similarly tie 2 overhand knots with cords 3 and 4.
Tie 2 overhand knots with cords 9 and 10, and 3 overhand knots with cords 11 and 12.
\*\*\* With cord 6 as leader, work a row of diagonal cording slanting to the left with cords 5, 4, 3, 2 and 1.
Work another row of cording immediately below with cord 5 as leader, and knotting over it cords 4, 3, 2, 1 and 6.
In a similar way, work a double row of diagonal cording slanting to the right, with cord 7 as first leader, and cord 8 as second leader, and knotting cords on right-hand side of motif over them.
Work a flat knot bead in centre of motif with cords 1, 2, 3, 4, 9, 10, 11 and 12. Use 2 outer pairs of cords as knotting cords, 4 central cords as knot-bearing core. Tie 4 flat knots before taking the sinnet up and over itself.\*\*
Work from \* to \*\* with second group of 12 cords.
Loop cord 8 of first motif round cord 5 of second motif to link them together, then let cord 8 continue as leader for first motif,

and work a row of diagonal cording slanting to the left knotting over it cords 7, 12, 11, 10 and 9.
Work a second row of diagonal cording immediately below with cords 7 as leader, and knotting over it cords 12, 11, 10, 9 and 8.
In a similar way work 2 rows of diagonal cording slanting to the right with left-hand part of motif, using cords 5 and 4 as leaders. Complete lower part of second motif in the same way.\*\*\*\*
Work 6 overhand knots with cords 1 and 2; 4 overhand knots with cords 3 and 4; 1 overhand knot with cords 5, 6, 7 and 8 (tie knot with double strands of cord); 4 overhand knots with cords 9 and 10; 6 overhand

knots with cords 11 and 12.
Work a similar overhand knot sequence with cords in second group of 12.
Repeat from *** to ****

**TO FINISH.** Trim ends to give fringe of required depth.

---

These are only a very few of the 'fancy' knots, and by no means represents the full extent of the knot vocabulary available to you. Much of the joy of macramé is in discovering – and inventing – new knots, to create a particular effect or add further embellishment to a pattern. The only limit to your knotting technique can be your own ability, imagination and of course your personal taste.

It is worth spending time searching through old nautical knotting manuals – you may well find a splendid fancy knot which could provide the perfect focal point to a piece of work.

*Unfinished fragment of knotting, English, early 20th century. First band of pattern shows cording leaf motifs and alternate half hitch chains. Below is a vandyke composed of closely-worked cording diamonds.*

# Finishing methods

So far all the samplers you have worked have ended in simple fringes, and this is of course by far the easiest way in which to end a piece of macramé work. Provided the knots in the last row are pulled fairly tightly, and the fringe trimmed evenly, the effect is pleasing to the eye and in keeping with the craft form.

Naturally however a fringe will not always be required, and other ways of finishing off your work should be practised: the method used will depend on the type of yarn you are working with, and the character of the knotting, but must in every case be neat and unobtrusive, and sufficiently secure to prevent the yarn unravelling.

The following methods will show you a few ideas; again, you will no doubt evolve new methods yourself to suit your work and yarn.

## COLLECTING KNOTS

This is an important category of knots which — as the name suggests — 'collect' groups of cords usually into tassels. Any knot which brings several cords together can be called a collecting knot, including a flat knot tied over multiple cords in order to regularise a pattern.

The pattern shown on page 107, top right, has been worked in alternate flat knots. To bring it to an attractive conclusion groups of 8 cords are combined: the 2 outer cords of each group are used to tie a flat knot over the 6 central cords, and the ends trimmed

evenly. This therefore would be termed a collecting knot.

An overhand knot can be used to collect ends in a similar way. The knot can either be tied in all the cords together or, if less bulk is wanted, one or two cords only knotted round the others.

*Evening bag has cords from back and front combined in collecting knots along lower edge.*

*Hanging 'Year In, Year Out' has ends collected in overhand knots along lower edge.*

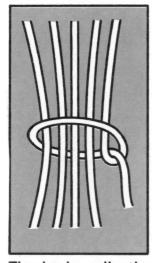

**The basic collecting knot (Note.** If a pattern simply instructs you to tie a collecting knot – or sometimes a gathering knot – this is the one to use). In any group of cords, the one on the far right is used to tie the knot. Form a loop in it where you want the knot to appear, then take the cord round the front of the group of cords from right to left, round the back of the group and through the loop. Draw it tight.

For extra strength, and also if a few horizontal coils are required to balance the tassel, work this knot several times over the group of cords, keeping the strands close together one below the other. This will create a similar appearance as the coil knot but of course will be on multiple cords, not single ones.

The same effect can be achieved by working the collecting knot with a separate cord rather than one of the set-on ends. The collecting cord can be mounted with a reversed double half hitch around the group of cords to be collected. You will then of course have 2 cord ends to work with. Either use both together to form loop and wrap around group of cords, as for basic collecting knot, or work knot with top cord of the pair only, and catching in lower one so it becomes part of the tassel. Alternatively simply wrap collecting cord tightly around group of cords so one end is caught and securely held, then finish wrapping with a basic collecting knot.

**Marling knot.** This collecting knot is derived from the overhand knot and is frequently found on fringes in nautical work. It is simply an overhand knot worked in one cord over another cord placed at right angles to it. It can be worked with multiple cords too, and in patterns with corners and angles.

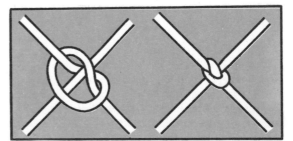

Place the knotting cord (or cords) under the knot-bearer, and at right angles to it. Take knotting cord up and over the knot-bearer,

then round itself from left to right and down through the loop formed. Draw tight.

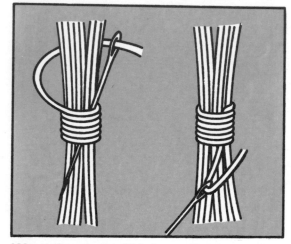

**Wrapping ends.** This is another very strong form of coil ending which can be used to collect several cords. Using one of the working cords, begin to wrap tightly around the group of cords from the point where you want the *bottom* of coil to occur, and wrapping upwards to the number of coils required. As you wrap, position a darning needle vertically, point down, against group of cords, and wrap over it.

When coil is complete, thread end of wrapping cord into the needle eye, and pull needle down through coil, bringing cord with it. Remove needle and you have a firm coil wrapping. Small coil knots can then be worked in individual cords, to give a neat, balanced finish.

## WEAVING IN

The tidiest method of concealing ends so you have no fringes, hanging cords or tassels but a perfectly smooth edge to your work is to weave in the loose ends on the wrong side. Ideally a pattern should finish with at least one row of cording as this gives a secure finish to the knotting, also as cording can be worked in any direction or shape it will give emphasis to your design.

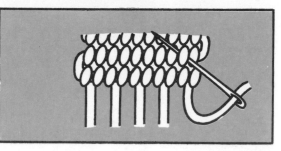

After the final row of cording turn work to the wrong side, thread each cord in turn on to a large-eyed darning needle, and weave ends through the last few rows of knotting. If the yarn is too thick to thread on to a darning needle, it will have to be carefully pulled through with a crochet hook.

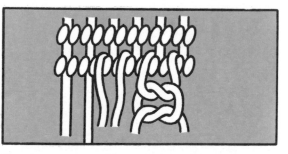

To give an even firmer finish after ends have been pulled through to reverse of work, provided they are evenly spaced across knotting, each pair of cords can be knotted together in 2-end flat knots (i.e. a flat knot without a central core).

## LINING WORK

This method is suitable for bags, garments and any items which will have to withstand a reasonable amount of wear and tear. Any item which is knotted in knitting or rug wool, or any heavy yarn, is best mounted on a fabric lining, as this will prevent the knots pulling or dropping out of shape. A complete fabric lining sewn to the wrong side of work will 'sandwich' all loose ends between the fabric and the knotting.

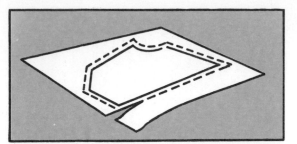

To make a lining, use the piece of finished knotting as a pattern. Lay knotting on top of fabric and cut round, adding ½ in. extra on all edges for seams (if wished a paper pattern can be made first, and then this pinned to fabric and the piece cut out to match).

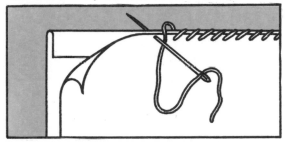

Place wrong side of fabric against wrong side of knotting, turning in ½ in. seam allowance on fabric. Stitch together, either machining close to edges, or using small neat overcasting hand stitches. The lining can either match or contrast with knotting yarn depending on the effect required.

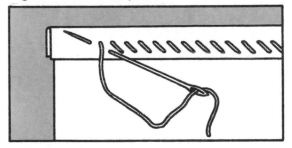

If a complete fabric lining is not a practicable proposition, or you prefer to retain the open-work character of your knotting, then the edges can be enclosed in seam binding. Cut binding to fit, pin it in place round edges, enclosing any loose ends, then machine stitch right round. Extra interest can be added to work by binding with tape in a contrasting colour to knotting yarn.

If the tape is not wished to be visible in finished work, place it right sides facing to

macramé, machine stitch as close to the edge as possible, then turn tape carefully to the wrong side and hemstitch neatly in place.

## GLUING ENDS

Some yarns – usually the strong linens and parcel strings which hold the knots well, and do not slip or fray – can merely be trimmed about an inch from the end of work, then turned to the wrong side and secured to the back of knotting with a spot of colourless fabric glue. The chess set on page 72 worked in dyed parcel string, has been ended in this way, the string trimmed and tucked inside the bottom of each piece, then lightly glued. Sometimes a combination of weaving and gluing may be required to keep ends neatly and securely concealed.

## MOUNTING ON RODS OR RINGS

It is sometimes necessary – or preferable – to finish work in the same way as you started: e.g. if a belt has its cords set on to a ring, you may wish to end by mounting cords on another similar ring. Or if a hanging is mounted on a wooden rod or bar, then to finish it in the same way gives a pleasing symmetrical effect. This may be done either with reversed double half hitches or with flat knots.

### Reversed double half hitch method

Turn work so the lower edge is at the top, lay it flat on your working surface, and place ring or rod in position close to last row of knotting. Work over it with reversed double half hitches with each cord in turn.

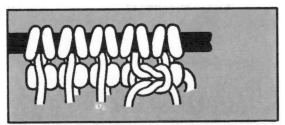

Finally, making sure all ends are on wrong side of work, turn work over and knot each pair of cords together in 2-end flat knots (i.e. no central core). Trim ends neatly.

## Flat knot method

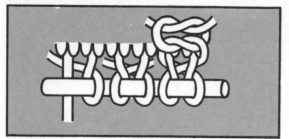

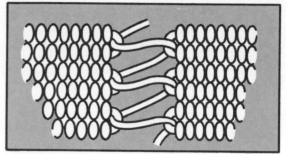

Turn work to wrong side, lay it flat on your working surface, and place ring or rod in position close to the last row of knotting. Working with cords in pairs, take them under and round rod, then behind themselves, cross them at the back and bring to the front again. Tie in a 2-end flat knot and trim close to edges. Secure with a spot of fabric glue on the knot itself, if required.

## JOINING SECTIONS OF KNOTTING

If you are working on an item in several sections which will later be combined – e.g. a dress, or bag – consider where the sections are to be joined, and if possible work these edges so the joining process will be simplified. For instance, if the two edges both finish with a row of flat knots then a further row of flat knots can be worked, combining one pair of cords from each edge.

In a cording pattern, small loops can be formed at the ends of each row with the leader cord, and these joined afterwards by lacing through the holes with a plain or knotted cord.

Fancy braids too can be used to combine sections of knotting – place the two edges side by side, and lay the braid centrally down the join. Stitch in place, using either neat overcasting stitches, or decorative embroidery stitches.

## OTHER METHODS OF FINISHING ENDS

Beads can be threaded on individual ends and overhand knots used to hold them in position. Or a row of overhand knots, or a single alternate half hitch chain worked on pairs of cords to stop them unravelling.

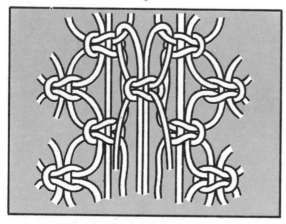

In an alternate flat knot pattern, a new pair of doubled cords (4 ends) can be added and knotted between the two edges, to continue the alternate flat knot pattern. Just lace the new cords through the looped edges of the sections to be joined, working a flat knot after each lacing, as shown in the diagram. In this method the join is virtually invisible.

*Three-colour hanging ends neatly with deep plain tassels.*

## TASSELS AND DECORATIVE CORDS

Collecting knots, as you have seen, can be used to collect ends into simple tassels. Sometimes a more dramatic tassel is required with a greater bulk of ends, and there are various methods of making these. Tassels can be worked directly on to the set-on cord ends, or can be made separately and attached when complete either to a macramé design or to any other fabric to form a decorative feature — round a lampshade edge, for instance, or as a cushion cover trimming. Tassels may be plain, or have a macramé patterned 'head'.

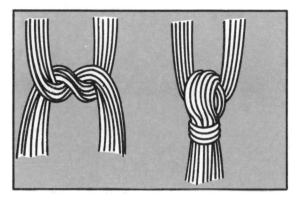

To work a plain tassel on set-on cord ends, divide cords into groups equal to the number of tassels required, then divide each group into two, and knot these two sets of cords together with the first half of a 2-end flat knot.

Now cut sufficient new lengths of cord to give the required bulk of tassel, each cord measuring a little over double the length of finished tassel. Pass these cords over the half knot, and tie a tight collecting knot with a separate cord round entire bundle of cords. This tassel has been used to end the blue and cream hanging, on page 90, and also the light pull on page 134.

A simple but effective variation on the plain tassel can be achieved by first tying each group of cords into a Josephine knot, then tying a half knot and adding a plain tassel as in previous method. This ending can also be added to a fabric item such as a linen table mat. Cords are set on all the way round hem edge as a fringed border, and then Josephine knots and tassels added as above.

To work a patterned tassel, cut about a dozen

cords (more or less depending on bulk of tassel required), each a little over double the required length of tassel. These are known as **filler cords**. Now cut the cords which will be used to work the knotted pattern: these should be approximately double the length of the filler cords, and should be in multiples of 4, 6 or 8 depending on the pattern you wish to work.

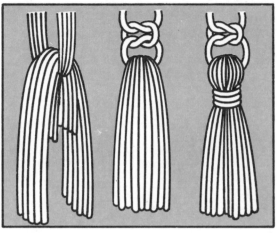

If adding tassel to cord ends of existing work, then tie ends together in groups with a half knot, as for previous methods, then fold knotting cords and filler cords together and loop over the half knot so knotting cords are above filler cords.

If making a separate tassel to attach to fabric or other item, loop a holding cord round bundle of filler and knotting cords and tie in a 2-end flat knot above bundle.

Work a collecting knot with 3 winds close to top of cords, just below the point where they have been attached to work or to holding cord. A separate cord or one of the knotting cords can be used to tie the collecting knot.

Now work whatever pattern you choose round knotting cords from the collecting knot down to a depth of about 2 in. (more or less depending on final finished length of tassel). Any knotting pattern may be used: the alternate flat knot pattern (you will need multiples of 4 cords for this); or diagonal cording; or a traditional leaf pattern.

If the pattern lends itself, a row of horizontal cording should be worked right round tassel to end, then all the cords trimmed evenly.

### Three patterned tassels to make

**Tassel 1** is suspended on a flat knot sinnet. Knotting cords are in a multiple of 4, and are worked in separate flat knot sinnets of 4 ends each to a depth of 2 in. A row of horizontal cording is worked round to finish and keep the sinnets in place.

**Tassel 2** is suspended on a three-strand plaited cord. Its knotting cords are in a multiple of 6, and a band of 6-knot leaf motifs are worked round. Horizontal cording to finish.

**Tassel 3** is suspended on a double alternate half hitch chain, has its knotting cords in a multiple of 4. The pattern is alternate flat knots, and is worked to a depth of 2 in. A row of horizontal cording completes the patterned 'head'.

### Decorative cordings

Each of the three tassels above, as you will see, has a patterned cord as a holding line: one is plaited, one a double alternate half hitch chain, one a flat knot sinnet. Any of these patterns may be used to make a decorative cord on its own — ends should be tied in overhand knots, to secure plaiting or knotting.

*Left to right: tassels 1, 2 and 3.*

To make a twisted cord, divide threads into 2 equal groups — only a few ends in each group for a thin cord; more for a thick heavy cord, depending of course on the yarn used. Obviously if a very thick yarn is used, 4 strands of it could well produce a far thicker cord than a dozen strands of a finer yarn. Twist each group of threads in a clockwise direction to form a long twisted cord. Then twist the 2 cords together in an anti-clockwise direction. Finish with an overhand knot to hold them together and prevent them from untwisting.

# Introducing colour

So far you have been working with only one colour of yarn at a time. The introduction of another colour – or colours – can add enormously to the interest and variety of a pattern.

Basically, there are two methods of working with colour: in the first method, when cords are set on they are arranged in a chosen colour sequence and thereafter by working any form of regular pattern, the colour effect produces itself. In the sampler which follows this section you will see how merely by arranging set-on cords in various dispositions of two colours, and then working exactly the same knotting pattern on each group, totally different effects can be achieved.

The second method is Cavandoli work which is based on a close cording technique. All the set-on cords are in the same colour, and the leader cord only is in the contrast colour. In this method you control the appearance and disappearance of the contrast colour as you work.

Dealing with method 1 first: try for a start setting on 8 threads, 4 in one colour, 4 in another contrasting colour. Arrange the colours alternately on the holding cord. Now work a straightforward alternate flat knot pattern – you will see at once the new dimension which has been added to the basic pattern (see illustration, page 107).

Next try working one or two simple sinnets or braids, and set on colour in any sequence preferred – use more than two colours if wished. Once the cords are set on you can forget about their colour and merely concentrate on working the knotting pattern. Try, for instance, setting on one cord in colour A, one cord in colour B (you then have 2

*Two belts worked in multi-colours. Cording takes colour from one side of work to the other.*

working ends in A; 2 in B). Work a tatted bar, as explained on page 61. Or working to the same colour sequence, try any of the half hitch variations shown on page 32. Compare these sinnets with the originals and you will see the instant dramatic difference a second colour makes.

For another two-colour braid, set on one cord in colour A, then set on a cord in colour B, setting it on the holding cord so one strand falls either side of the first cord. Now work a Solomon's bar with overhand knots, as explained on page 73.

Once cords have been set on in a particular colour sequence it is not necessary for the colour to remain in that part of the work. Again there are various methods of making colour disappear then reappear in an entirely different part of the work. Both cording and overhand knots can be used to make colour 'travel' in this way. In cording the important thing to remember is that the leader cord is always concealed in the finished knotting therefore a leader in colour A can be used to work horizontal or diagonal cording across cords in colour B, then whenever you wish colour A to reappear, the leader becomes a knotting cord and another cord is chosen as the leader.

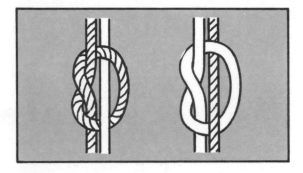

Similarly when overhand knots are tied in double cords, one cord knotting over the other, the colour which is shown in the finished work is the colour of the knotting cord. Therefore if cords are arranged in pairs, one each of colours A and B, wherever you want colour A to appear the A cord will knot over B cord; conversely when you wish colour B to appear, then the B cord becomes the knotting cord, and the A cord the knot-bearer.

The principal difference between these two colour control techniques is that with cording cords can physically travel to different parts of the work, but with overhand knots the colour only *appears* to travel: in fact the cords remain in their original set-on positions throughout. Colours can also be hidden in the centre of flat knot spirals or sinnets, and made to reappear by altering the sequence of knotting cords.

Before beginning a design using two or more colours it is as well to work out in rough where you want particular colours to appear, then devise a stitch pattern and colour control technique to suit. Time spent planning a colour project on paper, and working small samplers, will be well repaid in the final result.

If you work cording in a soft yarn such as knitting wool, rather than string, cotton or linen, the leader cord will always be completely hidden. Sometimes with the harder yarns, the leader is visible in odd spots.

The third coloured belt shown on page 144 is a good example of simple colour work — cords were set on in pairs of colours, and the alternate flat knot pattern used throughout. The belt shown at the top, on the other hand, demonstrates how colour is taken from one side of work to the other by means of cording.

The three belts on page 90, worked in dyed parcel string, show another use of cording in colour work, and a fascinating example of working in multi-colours in close diagonal cording throughout is shown in the pattern chapter, page 144.

The three-colour shawl pictured opposite demonstrates a technique where the coloured yarns stay more or less in the same place throughout the work. The curving of un-worked areas of yarn creates a pleasing feeling of movement.

The 18th century sampler on page 18 from the Victoria and Albert Museum shows seventy-five examples of knotting in multi-colours, most of the pieces intricately worked in very fine silks. This is a beautiful and impressive specimen and although not on general show at the Museum will be pro-duced on request.

In colour work it is not even necessary to work with yarns of similar weight: interesting textural effects can be achieved by com-bining different colours of totally different yarn types. The actual knots then take second place to texture and colour.

Berry knots are another useful device for transferring colour from one part of your work to another as the following sampler demon-strates.

*Opposite, top: three-colour shawl in fine knitting wool, in a simple diamond cording pattern. Below: multi-coloured heavy wool rug — sinnets of multi-end flat knots are arranged in an alternate pattern, with cording at top and bottom.*

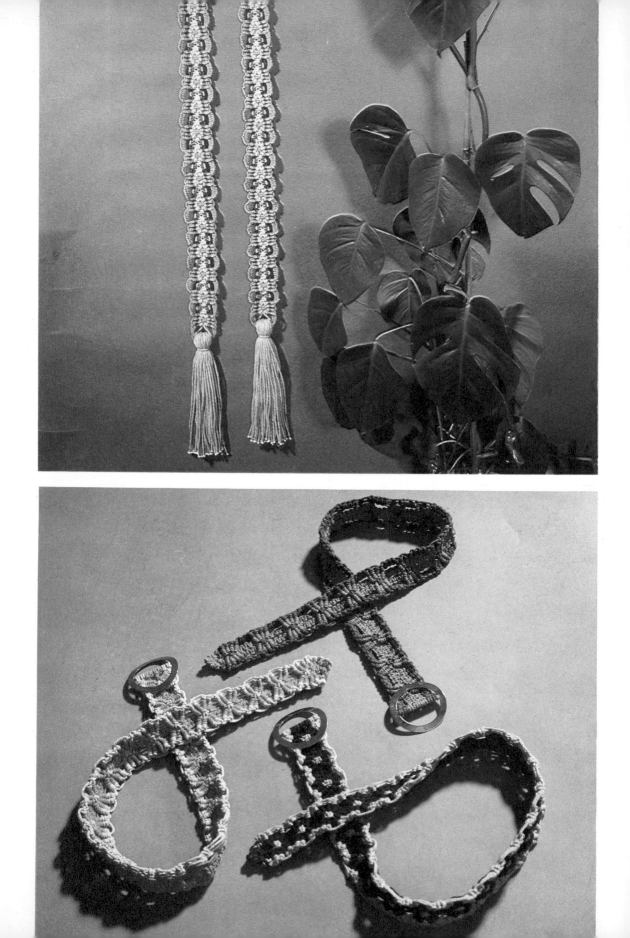

## Berry knot sampler

**YARN.** Medium string in two contrasting colours.

**MEASUREMENT.** Finished sampler measures approximately 3 in. square.

**PREPARATION.** Cut threads each 3 ft. long — 8 in colour A, 4 in colour B. Double them and set them with reversed double half hitches on to a holding cord about 18 in. long in the following order: 4 in colour A, 4 in colour B, 4 in colour A. You now have 24 working ends.

**TO MAKE.** * With first 8 cords make a berry knot, as explained on page 77.

Tie a multi-end flat knot with the next 8 cords: use 2 outer pairs of cords to knot, 4 central cords as knot-bearing core.

Work berry knot with last 8 cords.**

Link cords coming from lower right-hand corner of first berry knot with 4 cords coming from lower left-hand corner of multi-end flat knot as follows (cords are numbered from 1 to 8 for ease of identification):

Work vertical cording with cord 4 over cords 5, 6, 7 and 8 in turn.

Now cord 3 becomes a leader and cords 5, 6, 7 and 8 are knotted over it to form a row of cording immediately below the previous one.

Cord 2 then becomes a leader and a third row of cording is worked with cords 5, 6, 7 and 8.

Finally cord 1 is used to work vertical cording over cords 5, 6, 7 and 8 in turn. Work a similar sequence with cords coming from lower left-hand corner of second berry knot and cords coming from lower right-hand corner of multi-end flat knot.

Work berry knot in centre with the 8 cords in colour A.

Tie a multi-end flat knot with cords on either side of centre berry knot — i.e. one pair of colour A cords and one pair of colour B cords will be knotting cords, the knot-bearing core will have 2 colour A, 2 colour B cords.

Now work a similar 4-row cording motif as before in two colours, with cords coming

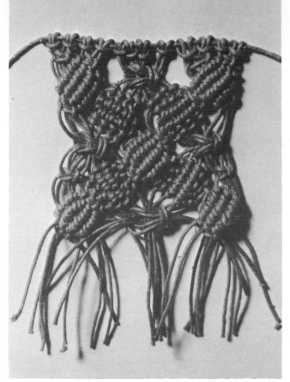

from lower left-hand corner of centre berry knot, and with cords coming from lower right-hand corner of first multi-end flat knot. Also work a similar motif with cords coming from right-hand lower corner of centre berry knot and with left-hand lower cords from second multi-end flat knot.

Repeat from * to **

**TO FINISH.** Trim ends to give fringe of required depth.

## Three-way colour sampler

The same knotting pattern is worked on each sampler on page 107 (bottom picture), yet they look totally different. This contrast is achieved merely by arranging cords in a different colour sequence each time.

## Sampler 1

**YARN.** Double knitting wool in two contrasting colours.

**MEASUREMENT.** Finished sampler measures approximately 6 in. long, excluding fringe.

**PREPARATION.** Cut 8 threads, each 64 in., 6 in colour A, 2 in colour B. Double them and set them with reversed double half hitches on to a holding cord (any colour)

*Opposite, top: hanging worked in three colours of dyed string. Diagonal cording creates an interesting, symmetrical colour pattern. Below: three belts also worked in dyed parcel string in a cording colour pattern.*

about 6 in. long. Arrange the cords in the following order: 1 in colour B, 6 in colour A, 1 in colour B. You now have 16 working ends.

**TO MAKE.** With cords 7 and 8, and 9 and 10 work a double alternate half hitch chain for 4 knots (2 from each side).
* Now take cord 1 as leader slanting down to the right to meet bottom of double alternate half hitch chain. Work diagonal cording over it with cords 2, 3, 4, 5, 6, 7 and 8.
Take cord 2 as leader and work another row of diagonal cording immediately below the previous one with cords 3, 4, 5, 6, 7 and 8. Similarly work 2 rows of diagonal cording slanting down to the left from the other side — i.e. cord 16 will be leader for first row of cording, cord 15 leader for second.
Work sinnet of 3 flat knots in centre of work with cords 2, 1, 16 and 15.
Work curved buttonhole bars (half hitches worked continuously from one side but eased to lie flat) as follows: knot 8 half hitches with cord 7 over cord 8, curving it as you work (see illustration on page 107). Work 16 half hitches with cord 5 over cord 6. Work 22 half hitches with cord 3 over cord 4.
Work 3 buttonhole bars with cords on right-hand side to correspond.
Using cord 2 as leader slanting to the left, work a row of diagonal cording from right to left, knotting over it cords 1, 8, 7, 6, 5, 4 and 3.
Work a second row of diagonal cording immediately below using cord 1 as leader, and knotting over it cords 8, 7, 6, 5, 4 and 3. At the end of this row knot 2 alternate half hitches with cords 1 and 2.
Work 2 similar rows of diagonal cording at right-hand side, but slant cording down to the right: use cord 15 as leader for first row, cord 16 as leader for second row.**
Knot cords 15 and 16 together with 2 alternate half hitches.
Work a double alternate half hitch chain with cords 7 and 8, and 9 and 10: 8 knots altogether (4 from each side).
Repeat from * to ** but do not tie half hitches in cords 1 and 2, and 15 and 16.

**TO FINISH.** Tie overhand knot in cords and trim to length required.

### Sampler 2

Make exactly as for sampler 1, but cut 4 threads in colour A, 4 in colour B. Set them on as follows: 2 in colour A, 4 in colour B, 2 in colour A. Proceed in same pattern as for sampler 1.

### Sampler 3

Make exactly as for sampler 1, but cut 4 threads in colour A, 4 in colour B. Set them on as follows: 4 in colour A, 4 in colour B. Proceed in same pattern as for sampler 1.

## CAVANDOLI WORK

The other basic method of two-colour knotting, Cavandoli work, is a particular form of macramé which was devised in Italy during the early part of the present century (see historical note, page 16). Worked in its traditional form in shades of natural, beige and brown, it closely resembles tapestry, and it is in fact sometimes hard to distinguish one from the other.

The principal difference between this technique and the colour knotting methods already described is that all the set-on cords for Cavandoli work are in the same colour, and the leader cord used throughout is in the contrast colour. Patterns are always worked in close cording, horizontal cording for the background of the piece, and vertical cording when the contrast colour is introduced. Cavandoli work is extremely flexible and once the technique has been mastered, intricate patterns representing figures, flowers, animals and all manner of geometric shapes can be worked.

The panel from the Cavandoli bag shown above (see also page 17) has a complex looking pattern representing men, horses, dogs and trees, yet it is fairly simple to work. The design is plotted in detail beforehand on graph paper, one square of the graph paper being equal to one knot in your work. Once a pattern has been planned it is a simple matter to follow the graph.

Although the principal attraction of Cavandoli work is the opportunity it offers for exciting colour designs, it can if wished be worked in a single colour only, with a pattern shape picked out in vertical cording. This

creates a pleasing textural effect totally different from other forms of knotting. See, for instance, the sampler right which is worked throughout in white cotton yarn on the Cavandoli principle.

*Above: panel from Cavandoli bag showing how design was worked in vertical cording. Below: Cavandoli work can be knotted in one colour, the knots themselves giving textural interest.*

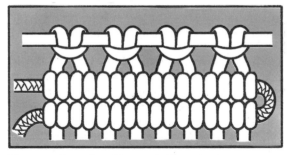

To practise the Cavandoli technique, set 4 cords in colour A on to a holding cord, and attach a separate leader in colour B at top left-hand corner. Work first 2 rows entirely in horizontal cording, colour A cords knotting over the colour B leader.

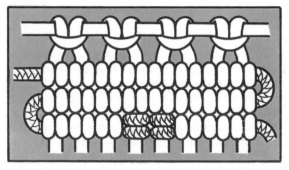

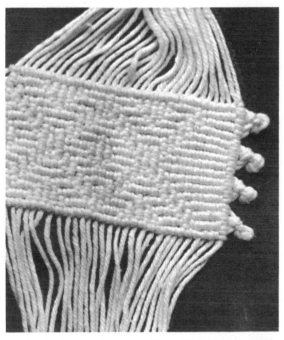

In the 3rd row, work horizontal cording with cords 1, 2 and 3, vertical cording is then worked with cords 4 and 5, so the leader becomes the knotting cord, and the base colour A cords the knot-bearers. Work horizontal cording with cords 6, 7 and 8.

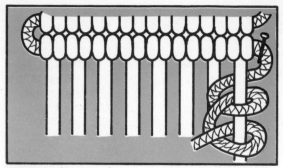

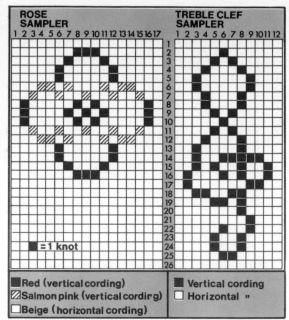

| ROSE SAMPLER | TREBLE CLEF SAMPLER |
|---|---|
| ■ = 1 knot | |
| ■ Red (vertical cording) | ■ Vertical cording |
| ▨ Salmon pink (vertical cording) | □ Horizontal ,, |
| □ Beige (horizontal cording) | |

If it is wished to change to the contrast colour at the beginning of a row, the leader cord is brought round a pin in the usual way, but immediately changes to become the knotting cord and vertical cording is worked with it over the set-on cords.

It is possible to work alternate blocks of colour by using the Cavandoli principle. For instance, set on 8 white cords to a holding cord (for practice purposes they should each be 1 yd. long); use a black cord approximately 4 yd. long as the leader.

**1st–4th rows:** * work 4 cords in horizontal cording (white), 4 cords in vertical cording (black)**; repeat from * to **.

**5th–8th rows:** reverse the colour sequence thus – * work 4 cords in vertical cording (black), 4 cords in horizontal cording (white)**; repeat from * to **.

**9th–11th rows:** same as 1st–4th rows.

**13th–16th rows:** same as 5th–8th rows.

Other colours can be introduced to Cavandoli work either by changing the leader cord where required or by setting on cords in different colours, but as the appeal of traditional Cavandoli lies mainly in the shapes created by vertical cording, to introduce colours in the horizontal cording could be confusing and may detract from the attractive simplicity of the technique.

A design motif may be outlined in the contrast colour, or may be filled in to give a solid shape. The two Cavandoli samplers shown on page 107, top picture, are both outline work.

These two samplers were both experiments in Cavandoli work, and the graphs on which the patterns were plotted are shown above. An important point to bear in mind when working out Cavandoli patterns is that in practice a design usually becomes slightly

elongated. This is probably due to the characteristic of the cording technique which involves a double knot, and therefore a double thickness of yarn. While the loops of the double half hitches sit snugly together in horizontal cording, in vertical cording the loops are positioned slightly apart – therefore one vertical half hitch will measure slightly more than one horizontal half hitch.

The rose pattern, for instance, appears fairly square looking on the graph – compare it with the photograph of the finished item and you will see how elongated the motif has become. Compensation can be made for this distortion by slightly extending the width of your chosen motif on the pattern graph.

The second sampler was one of my early efforts at Cavandoli work and not totally successful! It is intended to represent the musical treble clef symbol, and is worked with green garden twine on a fine macramé string base. The graph on which the pattern was planned is shown above. The main difficulty here was trying to produce curves from square knots!

An impression of curves can be created by graduating the introduction of the contrast colour in each successive row, but a motif such as this which depends so much on soft flexible curves is not easy to capture. Held at a distance, the symbol is just recognisable!

Once you have mastered the technique

you will be able to plot your own graphs. Remember always that one square on the graph equals one total knot (i.e. one complete double half hitch, horizontally or vertically), one complete row of squares reading across equals one complete row of cording.

## Rose Cavandoli sampler (see page 107)

**YARN.** Cotton knitting yarn in beige for background; double knitting wool in red and in salmon pink for design (or any two contrasting shades).

**MEASUREMENT.** Finished sampler measures 4 in. long, 2½ in. wide (excluding fringe).

**TENSION CHECK.** 5 rows of horizontal cording measure 1 inch long.

**PREPARATION.** Cut 9 cords in threads in background yarn, each 1 yard long. Double them and set them with reversed double half hitches on to holding cord (any colour) about 8 in. long (18 working ends).

**TO MAKE.** Attach a separate leader in red (or first contrast shade) to left-hand side of work, approximately 1 yard long. Now work from chart opposite. Numbers at the top refer to working cords; the numbers down the right-hand side refer to rows.

Work throughout in close cording, knotting horizontal cording with the set-on cords over leader cords for all the blank squares on chart. Change to vertical cording, knotting the red cord over set-on cords for all the marked squares.

When you reach row 6, change to a leader cord in salmon pink (or second contrast shade). Change back to red for rows 8–10 (inclusive); salmon pink for rows 11 and 12; and red for the remainder.

**TO FINISH.** Trim ends to form fringe. Trim leader cords and weave the ends into back of work.

*Macramé lace band, made in Italy in the late 16th century. Open-work diamonds of twisted chains alternate with triangles of flat knots.*

# Knotting in the round

All the knotting patterns given so far have been worked flat to a more or less rectangular shape but it is perfectly easy to work macramé 'in the round', or in tubular form. This working technique is the basis for most three-dimensional macramé sculptures and hangings. It also allows garments to be made without any bulky side seams, but in one perfectly smooth piece.

The basic technique is simple: instead of setting threads on to a length of yarn laid flat on your working surface, the holding cord is first joined into a circle of suitable size and the threads are set on to this.

Of course you can no longer use a flat board as a working surface, but will have to adapt various shapes and sizes of bases to suit your work. I find an upturned china pudding basin covered with a padding of foam plastic makes a good base for 'in-the-round' knotting, and as I have pudding basins in a variety of sizes there is usually one to suit the item I am making. The plastic basins are not good as they tend to be too light (unless suitably weighted).

A thick glass flower vase, suitably padded, can also work well, so can solid rubber balls, a circular biscuit tin padded on the outside and filled inside with a heavy weight, an upturned paint pot, or a piece of wood cut to the exact size and shape required.

If you are making a hat then a wig stand is the ideal base on which to work, as you can be sure the hat will fit! Have a look round the house – and garage – and you are bound to find several suitable articles to use for bases. Remember always to pad the base with foam plastic, towelling, felt or any other soft surface if you want to pin your work as you knot.

As the holding cord will no doubt form an important part of the finished design – e.g. the top edge of a bag, or the neckline of a poncho or blouse – it is essential it is strong enough to bear the weight of the completed knotting. It is often a good idea to set threads over a double or even triple holding cord.

The chess set, pictured on page 72 and opposite, was worked in the round. Threads were set on to a holding cord cut and tied into a circle of the appropriate size for each piece, then the alternate flat knot pattern worked throughout to form a straight tubular shape. The basic pattern of the bigger pieces – king, queen, knight and bishop – was embellished with flat knot loops to indicate the relative importance of each piece in the game. When knotting was complete, cords were trimmed, the ends tucked inside each piece, and secured with a spot of glue.

## TUBULAR WORK

The simplest method of working in the round is merely to set on your threads to a circular holding cord, as described above, then work any knotting pattern on the set-on cords in the usual way. Work can be shaped as you knot by easing the knots, slackening or tightening them as required. This is why it is essential to have a working base more or less tailormade to the size and shape of the finished item, otherwise shaping becomes a matter of guesswork.

If the piece is to remain tubular (i.e. open at both ends), then the ends can be finished by any of the methods used for flat work. If however it is necessary to have the tube closed at the bottom (e.g. for a bag) then in the final row – or rows – the cords are combined in pairs across work.

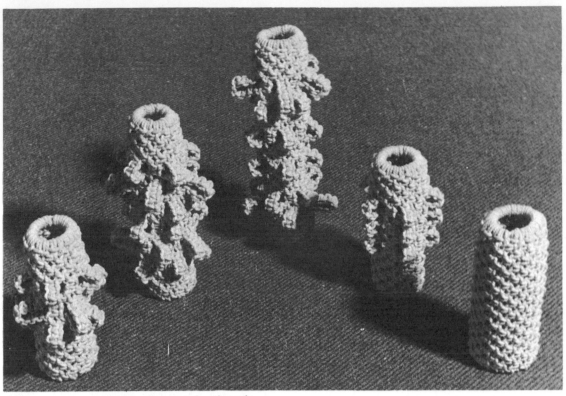

*Chess set was worked in the round — threads were set on to a top circle of string.*

Remove work from the base, and lay it on your flat working surface, positioning the work so it lies evenly, and in the shape and arrangement of finished item. Now, working from left to right, knot cords together combining cords from the front with cords from the back: e.g. to knot in flat knots, knot cords 1 and 2 from the front over cords 1 and 2 from the back — and so on right across the row.

Of course any knotting technique can be used provided it combines the cords neatly and gives a sufficiently firm finish to the work. Bags are often completed after the final row of combined knots by adding fringes or tassels. Most of the bags in the pattern section have been worked in the round, and the cords combined along the lower edge. Have a look at them — and the others illustrated through the book — and note the various knotting techniques which have been used to combine the cords.

## STARTING FROM THE CENTRE

Another method of working in the round is to start in the centre and work outwards and round. This technique can be used to produce a flat piece of work, such as a medallion mat, or square number 3 illustrated on page 144, or it may be shaped as you work to produce three-dimensional designs such as a hat or a tea-cosy.

If you intend to work on a shaped design then you will need a three-dimensional working surface, but if you are working on a flat design then you can use your normal flat working surface.

There are four methods of setting on cords when working from the centre.

### Method 1

Set a number of threads on a holding cord, then overlap ends of holding cord and set on more cords over the double thickness. Tighten holding cord until it is the required size, and space the set-on cords equally round the circle adding more if needed. Pin to working surface and knot in chosen pattern.

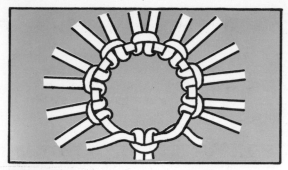

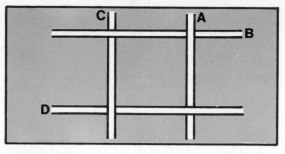

## Method 2

Set cords directly on to a wooden, plastic, metal or rubber ring. This gives a firm beginning to your work.

## Method 4

This method starts with a square of cording in the centre. Lay 4 leather cords in a criss-cross square, as shown in the diagram, above.

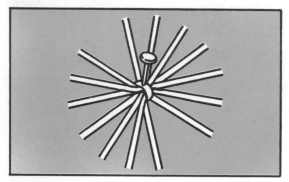

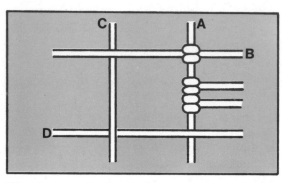

## Method 3

Cut required number of cords and tie them together round the centre with a small length of yarn. Pin them through centre holding cord (knot side down) to working surface and space out cords in a wheel pattern.

Working on leader A first: set on a double thread with reversed double half hitches (cording), positioning it in centre of leader A. Now work cording over leader A with leader B, close to the set-on threads.

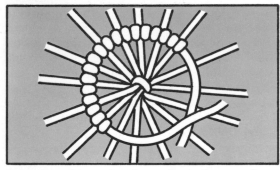

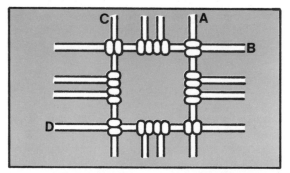

Now introduce a leader a short distance from centre point and overlap ends to form a circle. Work cording over it with each cord in turn. Continue in chosen knotting pattern. This method is suitable for an item where it is wished to add a pompon or other form of decoration to the centre point afterwards. The collected group of cords in the centre gives a base on which to stitch a decoration.

In a similar way set on a doubled thread to centre of leader B, then work cording over B with leader C. Set on a doubled thread to centre of leader C, work cording over C with leader D. Finally set on a doubled thread to centre of leader D, and work cording over D with leader A to link the square together. Knotting continues on these cords in chosen pattern, working outwards.

## Adding new cords

Unless you are knotting a very open-work pattern, you will almost certainly wish to add new cords when working out from the centre.

The easiest and most unobtrusive method of introducing new cords is to insert circular leaders and work cording over them with existing cords, at the same time setting on new cords where required with the double half hitch (i.e. *not* the reversed double half hitch as normally used for setting on, but the cording form of the knot — see diagram, above). Careful pinning will be needed to keep work flat and the knotting regular.

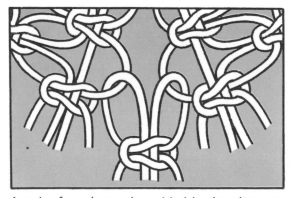

A pair of cords can be added in the alternate flat knot pattern merely by looping over the existing cords at the point where the new cords are required (see diagram, above), and then tying in a flat knot.

If you are working on a hat, or design which requires gentle shaping as well as extra cords, then ease knots by tightening or slackening over working surface to produce the required effect. Careful pinning will help to give a regular even shape. Metal, plastic or wooden rings can be added at any point in your work to give extra rigidity and stability to the item.

## TUBULAR CORD SAMPLER

This two-colour tubular cord is made by a unique but very simple knotting technique based on close cording. The tube is hollow and has spirals of colour around it — if wished four different colours of yarn can be used to give a multi-coloured effect. Try making the tube in different yarns for different purposes — fine knitting yarn, for instance, will give a soft, floppy tube which can be used as a tie cord, but parcel string will give a completely rigid tube which will stand by itself. When the tube is complete it is impossible to tell where the knotting began. The technique is very effective, satisfying to work — and yet perfectly simple to do.

**You will need:** 12 knotting cords, 6 of colour A, 6 of colour B, and 3 leader cords — the length of knotting cords will of course depend on required finished length of tube but each knotting cord should be approximately 4 times the finished length. Leader cords should be about the same length, and can be in any colour as they will not show in finished work.

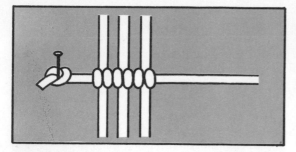

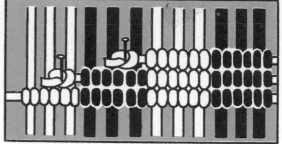

**To make tube:** lay 3 cords in colour A on working surface. (**Note.** The cords are not doubled this time, but mounted singly.) Tie an overhand knot in one end of first leader and pin it to the left of the 3 cords, about 4 in. down from cord ends. Work double half hitches with each cord over the leader to form a row of close cording.

Now lay the final 6 cords, 3 in colour A, 3 in colour B, to the right of the double row of cording. Pin leader 3 to working surface to the left of the new cords, and immediately above double row of cording. Work cording across the 6 cords with leader 3. Then work cording across the 6 cords with leader 2, and finally a third row of cording on the 6 cords with leader 1.

You should now have 3 graduated rows of cording, as in diagram, above. Remove from the working surface and join into a ring by working cording with all 12 cords over leader 3.

**Next round:** work cording with all 12 cords over leader 2.

**Next round:** work cording with all 12 cords over leader 1.

Continue in this way. As you complete each round you will find a leader lying ready placed for the next round. Continue until tube is the required length.

Tie cords at beginning and end into overhand knots to form 2 equal tassels, or if no loose ends are wanted, trim cords, tuck them into tube and secure with a spot of glue.

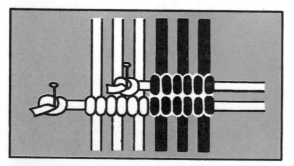

Now lay 3 cords in colour B to the right of the row of cording just worked. Pin leader 2 to the working surface with an overhand knot positioning it on the left of the colour B cords, and immediately above the row of worked cording.

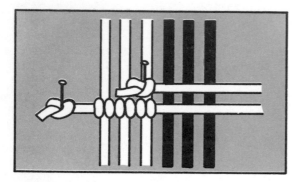

Work a row of double half hitches with each colour B cord over leader 2. When that row is complete, work another row of cording with colour B cords over leader 1.

# Headings and edges

## DECORATIVE HEADINGS

As the set-on edge of your work often forms an important part of the finished design, sometimes a more ornate beginning than a plain straight line is wanted. There are various ways of setting on threads to give decorative headings, and the particular version selected should of course be in keeping with the rest of the pattern, complementing it rather than conflicting with it. Most of these headings are based on various forms of picots (loops).

### Simple picot edging

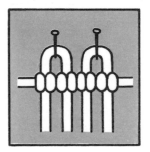

Threads are set on double as usual but instead of setting on by the reversed double half hitch, lay the doubled thread under holding cord, with the looped end extending fractionally beyond holding cord. Work a double half hitch with left-hand thread over the holding cord, pin the top loop to working surface then work a double half hitch with right-hand thread over holding cord. The size of the picot depends on how far you let the top loop of the set-on thread extend beyond holding cord. The picture, below, shows how the size of the picot can be varied. Working double half hitches without the picot loops to set on threads is useful when introducing new threads in a row of cording, as it is then virtually impossible to tell where the new threads were added.

### Overhand picot edging

Begin as for simple picot edging, by working a double half hitch with left-hand thread, then tie an overhand knot in the top loop immediately above the holding cord, and complete mounting with a double half hitch worked with right-hand thread. Alternatively, before doubling thread and pinning it to working surface, tie an overhand knot in the centre of it, then pin it in place to

*Left to right: simple picot edging (small and large); overhand picot; chain picot; 4 versions of the flat knot picot; simple scalloped edge; half hitch, tatted and chain scallops.*

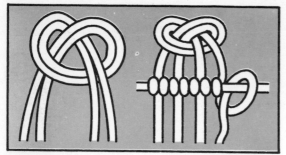

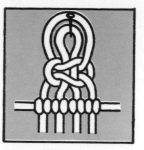

working surface, lay holding cord across it just below overhand knot, and work double half hitches with left- and right-hand threads. This method ensures that the overhand knot is close to holding cord.

## Chain picot edging

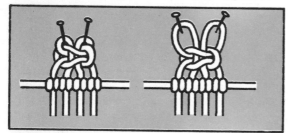

Double the thread and work an alternate half hitch chain from the fold down to the required depth, then attach thread to the holding cord with double half hitches.

## Flat knot picot edging

There are various methods of working this edging, depending on the effect required.

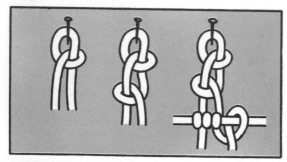

**Method 1.** Double 2 threads and lay them side by side on working surface, pinning loops in place. Now tie a flat knot, knotting outer threads over central inner ones. Attach to holding cord by working double half hitches with each of the 4 threads coming from the flat knot. This gives a neat twin looped edging.

**Method 2.** Double 2 threads as before, but this time pin to working surface positioning one cord inside the other so you have a double loop at the top. Work flat knot as before, and attach to holding cord with double half hitches.

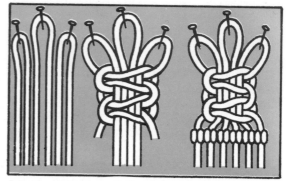

**Method 3.** A trefoil edging can be working by using 3 double threads. Pin them to the working surface as shown, left, so centre loop is slightly higher than the outer loops. Tie a flat knot, knotting outside threads over centre core of 4 threads. Attach to holding cord with double half hitches across all threads.

A deeper edging can be made by working a sinnet of flat knots from any of these picot beginnings before attaching to holding cord.

## Simple scalloped edge

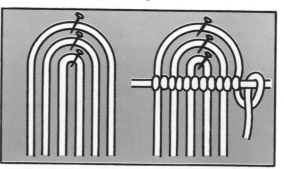

Double 3 threads and pin them to the working surface, each inside the other to give a triple loop at the top. Lay holding cord over them and work double half hitches across.

## Half hitch scalloped edge

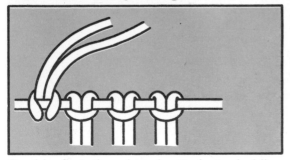

Double first thread and attach to holding cord with a reversed double half hitch so cords are hanging in the opposite direction from work, and the knot of the reversed double half hitch is on the wrong side. Set on 3 threads by the reversed double half hitch with their cords hanging the correct way.

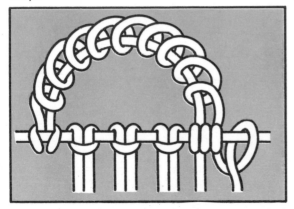

Now work half hitches with cord 1 over cord 2 curving the chain round as you work to form a scalloped edge above the 3 set-on threads. When scallop is as deep as you wish, attach to holding cord with double half hitches, thus bringing cord ends down into the rest of the work. More or fewer threads can be set on between scallop depending on how wide you wish scallop to be.

## Tatted scalloped edge

Set on as for half hitch scallop, but work the scallop with reversed double half hitches (tatted bar).

## Chain scalloped edge

Set on as for half hitch scallop, but work the

*Lampshade in a free pattern of fine silky yarn — threads were set on to one of the frame's struts, and knotting worked sideways round frame.*

scallop in an alternate half hitch chain. For a chunkier scallop, set on 2 threads together and work a double alternate half hitch chain.

These decorative edgings are particularly attractive when working in the round, and the set-on edge will form the opening of a bag, or the neckline of a dress or blouse.

## ALTERNATIVE BEGINNINGS

Do not feel you have always to begin work by setting threads on to a holding cord, or a rod or ring. Depending on the item you are making, many other ways can be devised to suit the particular article. Belts, chokers and bracelets, for instance, which involve only a few cords can be started by merely tying an overhand knot in cords a few inches from the end to form a tassel. Work then progresses in the chosen knotting pattern, and is finished with another overhand knot. Ends are trimmed so the tassels are both the same length.

Another way to begin a belt is shown on

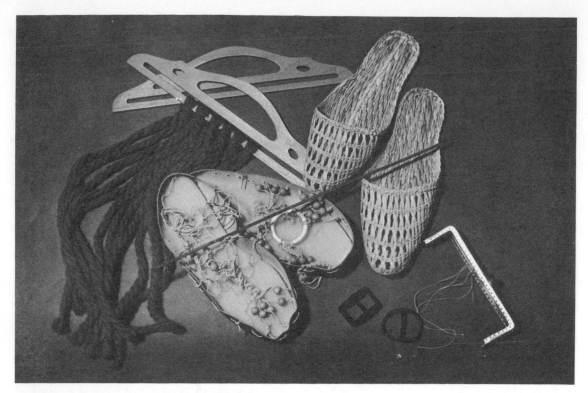

*Threads may be set directly on to bag or purse frames, shoe soles or buckles.*

page 141. Here individual flat knot sinnets were first worked and the sinnets combined with a row of linking flat knots, then work continued on main knotting pattern. An overhand knot or a row of cording could have linked the sinnets equally satisfactorily, or the sinnets could be worked in alternate half hitch chains.

If you want a looped start, which is useful as a fastening device for a bracelet or belt, double cords in the usual way, and lay them on your working surface so each cord is inside the other to give a multiple top loop. Now tie a flat knot with outer cords over central core. Alternatively the cords could be tied with an overhand knot, but this will give a less flat loop.

It is not always wished to work from a narrow end downwards. A necklace, for instance, or sometimes a belt can have a series of short threads set on a holding cord sufficiently long to go round neck, or waist. The design is then worked down to the depth required.

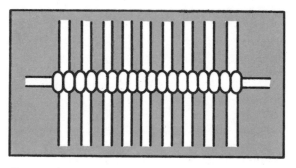

Remember too that threads do not have to be set on doubled although this is often the most convenient method. If you want a matching fringe at the beginning and the end of your work, set threads on singly by double half hitches on to a holding cord, leaving yarn to extend above holding cord to measurement of fringe required. Finish work by knotting a row of cording across, and trim ends to match fringe at the beginning.

**Note.** When threads are set on singly they need only be cut 4 times the finished length required (see assessing yarn quantities, page 111).

Threads may also be set directly on any bought accessory such as handbag or purse handles, on shoe soles if holes are punched round edges, on lampshade frames — and so on. In the lampshade shown on page 103 threads were set on to one of the frame's side struts. The very free pattern was knotted round the shade with cording worked over every side strut and eventually knotting was linked to the originally set-on threads. A second outer layer of 'floating' cords was then added by setting threads on to top circle of lampshade frame, and the threads taken down diagonally and secured to lower circle of frame.

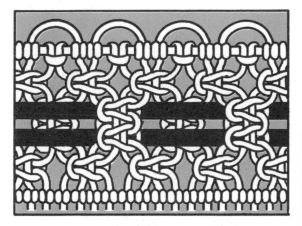

A drawstring edge can be useful for a bag or dress. Set threads on to a holding cord, preferably with a decorative heading (see pages 101–3), then work a row of flat knots. Work individual short sinnets of flat knots between knots of previous row to depth required for drawstring, then work a single row of flat knots between the sinnets and continue in chosen knotting pattern.

Alternatively pin cut threads to your working surface and knot each set of 4 cords in flat knot sinnets. When sinnets are long enough, unpin them, fold them over and combine cords from the beginning with working cords by tying 8-end flat knots. Now link looped sinnets by a single row of flat knots worked between sinnets — i.e. 2 outer left-hand cords of each sinnet will be linked with 2 outer right-hand cords of sinnet on the left. Continue in chosen knotting pattern. If wished the flat knot sinnets can be looped over a rod or bag handle before tying in the 8-end flat knot.

## Starting in the centre

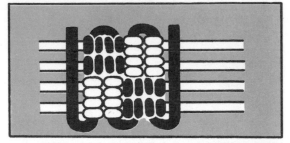

Very heavy work — a rug for instance — can sometimes be difficult to manage if started from one end. In this case knotting may commence in the centre of the proposed pattern and this too will help to eliminate the problem of working with excessively long ends. If using a cording pattern, lay cut threads on working surface, and place a leader cord at right angles across centre of threads. Knotting can now progress in both directions, as shown in the diagram.

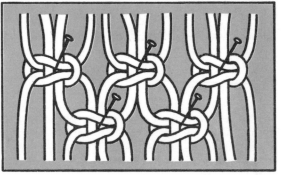

If working a flat knot pattern merely select the midway point on the cut threads, and work a row of flat knots across. Continue working on either side of this first row. Careful pinning will again help to keep work regular and knotting even.

By working from the centre out for an item such as a belt, it is easier to control the length — especially if the pattern is not a regular all-over one. When it involves a motif, for instance, which has to be positioned exactly in the centre of the belt, it is not always easy to gauge this precise position if you start work from one end. If you start in the centre however you begin with the motif and work out symmetrically on either side of it.

## A turned mounting

This method of mounting forms a cording braid at the top of your work which gives a particularly firm edging.

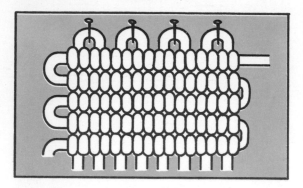

Begin with a number of doubled cords — our sample piece uses 4. The exact number will depend on width of braid required. Pin these cords by their loops to your working surface and set on to a leader cord with simple picot heading. Now work rows of close horizontal cording, over the leader cord, but allow leader to form picot loops along one side of the braid, as shown in the diagram. Continue until length of braid is equal to width of finished article, finish knotting and cut cords.

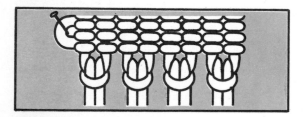

Turn work and pin to working surface so the side picot loops are now at the bottom of braid. Set on threads to each picot with a reversed double half hitch and continue work in chosen knotting pattern.

Alternatively when working the close cording attach a new leader after every 2 rows, leaving ends dangling, then when work is turned, these ends will become the knotting cords for main pattern.

Some more ideas for starting work with a shaped edge will be found in the chapter on shaping, page 118.

## DECORATIVE EDGES

Knotting patterns, however attractively worked and neatly finished, can be spoiled if the sides of the piece have not received the same care and attention. This is particularly true of square designs, or any sort of symmetrical pattern where one side must balance the other.

You have already learned how to start your work with decorative picots and scallops, and you have learned a variety of ways to finish designs. The sides of work however present special problems of their own: if you are working with a continuous leader, it is only too easy for it to get pulled either too tightly or left too slack, and so create an untidy messy look to the beginning and end of the rows. Careful and consistent pinning at the end of each row to change direction of the leader should help to regularise the knotting.

In the alternate flat knot pattern, the rows where the end cords are left unworked again requires precise pinning so the amount of loop allowed in the unworked cords is consistent every time, and in keeping with the rest of the pattern. If you are working a close alternate flat knot pattern, for instance, then these outer cords should be pulled equally tightly. On the other hand if the pattern is a loose open one, then the outer cords must be correspondingly open as well.

Usually whichever variety of pattern is being worked, it is best to allow the first and last cords of the row to form loops, but to pull the second and penultimate cords fairly tightly downwards. If both cords are allowed to loop this gives an untidy floppy look to the edge of the work. After the first knot in the subsequent row has been worked gently pull the central core cords and this will tighten the second cord of the row. Similarly with the last knot in the row, if you pull core cords the penultimate cord of the row will be tightened.

Very often a knotting pattern is taken right to the side edges so the problem of a decorative border does not arise. Sometimes however it is wished to contain a central motif with an edging which continues round

*Opposite, top: rose Cavandoli sampler, treble clef Cavandoli sampler, alternate flat knots in two colours. Below: three-way colour sampler.*

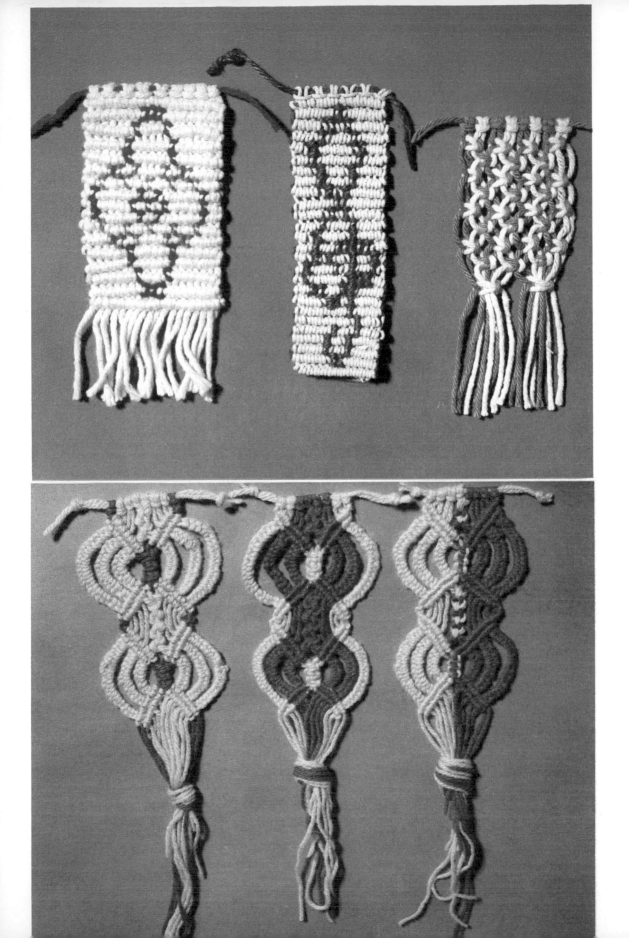

the sides as well as at top and bottom. Such an edging can be worked in with the main pattern, or may be added afterwards in the form of a fringe or a braid. Alternatively, a braid can be worked first, then pinned to your working surface and knotting cords looped into it as you work (see bikini pattern, page 164).

If you are working in cording, allow the leader cord to form a small picot (loop) at the end of each row, as it turns to begin the next. Then it is easy afterwards to set on new cords to these picots to form a plain or knotted fringe.

The cords for the main pattern can also be set on with picots and the work ended by creating similar picots: loop each end back on itself, weave ends through back of work. Remember however that one picot on the set-on edge represents two working ends, so the finishing picots should only be worked on alternate cords; non-picot cords should be taken straight to the back of work and woven or darned in. With picots on all four edges, a matching fringe can then be set on to give a pleasant symmetrical appearance to the finished work.

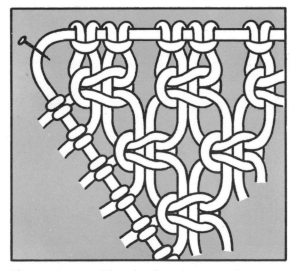

If you are working in the alternate flat knot pattern, and are decreasing at the sides —

*Opposite: glove puppet — a delightful blend of many different needlework techniques. Yoked cape is trimmed with macramé sinnets worked in embroidery silks.*

either gradually, or sharply to a point — you will have a series of loose ends right down the shaped edge (see chapter on shaping, page 118). These can be neatly finished, and at the same time given a decorative firm edge with diagonal cording. The holding cord should be left long at both sides when setting on threads. When main knotting is complete, unpin holding cord and untie overhand knots, insert pins to working surface alongside first and last knots, then bring holding cords round pins to form leaders for diagonal cording down side edges.

If shaping does not start immediately below set-on edge, weave holding cords through at ends of rows until shaping point is reached then take round a pin and begin diagonal cording. If cording is to be worked round entire edge, it is probably neater to use the holding cord from one side only as leader, taking it from one top corner all the way round and up to opposite top corner. It can then be unobtrusively woven into the back of the set-on edge.

### Cording edges for a square

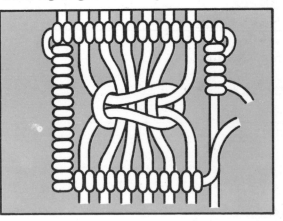

The central pattern of a square design can be 'contained' by working a row of horizontal cording at the beginning and end, and vertical cording down the sides. Ends of the leader from horizontal cording should be left long enough to become knotting cords for the vertical cording down outer cords at each side. After vertical cording is complete, one of the two knotting cords can then become leader for final row of horizontal cording. Its end can be woven into the back of vertical cording at opposite side and so link the four sides of the cording border together.

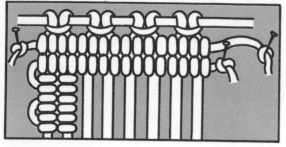

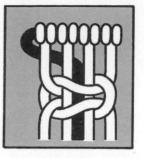

Because of the nature of vertical cording, where the knotting cord is continually being reversed and the loop of each reversal is difficult to hide, sometimes it is neater to work double rows of cording. In this case at the end of the first row of horizontal cording, leave leader pinned to the working surface out of the way of knotting, and introduce a new leader for second row. At the end of this row the leader then becomes the knotting cord for the vertical cording worked on the first and second cords.

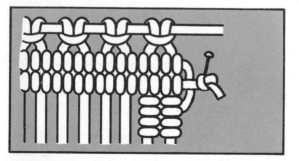

Unpin the leader at the end of first row of horizontal cording and weave it through back of second row bringing it out just below end of second row. It then becomes knotting cord for vertical cording on last 2 cords. When vertical cording is complete, work 2 rows of horizontal cording using knotting cord from left-hand vertical cording as leader. The knotting cord from right-hand vertical cording can be trimmed and the end woven into the wrong side of horizontal cording to neaten.

Any sinnet of flat knots, or half hitches, or reversed double half hitches, can be used to 'frame' a piece of work at the edges, creating straight lines which can help to regularise a design, especially where a complex central knotting pattern is used.

If you are working a pattern where bands of alternate flat knots are separated by frequent rows of cording, to introduce a new leader on every cording row will leave a number of untidy loose ends at the sides. These can be 'decorated' with beads (see page 124), thus making a virtue of a necessity! But if a neat uncluttered finish is preferred, then on each flat knot row, the leader from cording can be taken into knot-bearing core of first or last knot (depending on position of leader cord), sandwiching it between the other 2 central cords. When it is required as a leader again, it is simply brought back to the end of the row and taken round a pin ready to begin cording.

# Coping with technical problems

## LEARNING THE QUALITIES OF YARN

You should by this time be reasonably familiar with a variety of different yarn types and qualities, and be able to appreciate the particular characteristics of each. Try now going back to some of the early samplers or knotting patterns in the book, and making each up in a different yarn from the one you originally used. You will be astonished at the entirely new effects you achieve.

The pictures below, for example, show exactly the same pattern made up three times, but sampler A is in fine rayon, sampler B is in synthetic tubular cord, sampler C in extra thick Orlon. This experiment also illustrates the importance of checking 'tension' before embarking on a finished piece of work — as you can see there is a vast difference between the size of sampler A and the size of samplers B and C!

Knitting and crochet patterns as a rule give a guide to the important factor of tension, for it is tension which controls the finished size of your work and especially when making a garment it is vital that you achieve the correct tension otherwise the garment will never fit.

Macramé patterns tend not to be able to give such precise information, mainly because of the flexible nature of the work, and because so many different yarn types can be used. Generally however an indication of the finished size, or of one complete motif of the pattern will be given, and it is essential before you embark on the complete item that you check this measurement by working a small sample of the knotting pattern in the yarn you want to use.

If, for example, your chosen yarn makes up to a motif only 2 in. square, and the pattern indicates a motif of 4 in., you know you will have to work twice as many motifs if you want to end up with work of the correct total size.

Also keeping a detailed and accurate record of your work, and the yarns used, will help to save time with tension checking. If you already have sizes and results noted to which you can refer you may not have to work a sample piece. The trouble taken with such details is always worth while: in the long run it can prevent hours of lost time, and money wasted on expensive yarns.

## ASSESSING YARN QUANTITIES

To assess the exact quantity of yarn required for a macramé project, and the lengths of individual cords, is one of the most difficult

*One pattern, three yarns. Lower right-hand corner: fine rayon (sampler A); above: synthetic tubular cord (sampler B); left: extra thick Orlon (sampler C).*

111

*Rug in thick piping cord is worked in an
alternating pattern of banister bars.*

aspects of the craft. Until now the subject has been deliberately avoided, as specific yarn lengths have been given for samples, and for practice purposes. However when you embark on planning your own designs it is essential to have some sort of guide-line to work to. As you will have seen by the previous section on experimenting with different yarn, some yarns – the thicker, harder ones – get used up much quicker in knotting than the soft fine ones.

Again, too, your record of work should note information about yarn quantities, and how much yardage to allow for a particular project. Joining in new cords in the middle of your work is not always satisfactory, although there are methods available (see page 116). Ideally individual yarn ends should be cut to exactly the length required to take them right through the work. It is better therefore always to over-estimate lengths required.

However you do not want to waste good yarn unnecessarily by cutting over-long ends – for when the cords are trimmed afterwards the short ends are usually not much use for anything other than holding cords. Again, keeping a detailed record will save you time and money.

As a very general rule of thumb, cords should be cut to approximately eight times the length of finished article (i.e. when set on double each working end will be equal to four times the finished length). If you wish to produce work measuring 1 yd., for instance, you will cut cords to 8 yd. each. When they are set on, working ends will each measure just under 4 yd.

On the whole, assuming the knotting pattern is fairly evenly divided over total number of cords, this assessment works out reasonably well. However if a pattern is used where particular cords are used all the time to knot, and others are consistently knot-bearers – e.g. in flat knot sinnets, or vertical cording – the knotting cords will quickly get used up.

In time you will learn to be able to judge from a pattern which cords are going to be used up quickly, and which can be cut shorter because they are mainly used only as knot-bearers. The choker on page 145, for instance, is worked on outer cords which are cut considerably longer than the inner ones, as the pattern is a regular one throughout, and the inner cords are never at any time used to knot.

Similarly, a design which uses many areas of unworked or floating cords (such as the rope belt on page 142) will obviously not require such long cords as one with a closely worked knotting pattern.

The shawl on page 155 demonstrates another instance where careful assessing of yarn quantities before embarking on a project will save you cutting excessively long cords. This pattern is based on the triangle principle, where only the centre 2 threads are cut to the full length (e.g. approximately 8 times the required finished length). These threads are set on first to the holding cord, then other threads set on either side of the central ones, their lengths gradually decreasing each time up to the top corners of the triangle. Approximately 4 in. can be allowed for each decrease, but again there will be variation with different yarns.

When working a triangle in the alternate flat knot pattern, the depth of the triangle will be pre-determined by the number of set-on threads, and not something you can decide as you work.

As a very general guide, the depth of the triangle is approximately equal to half the measurement of the set-on edge. For example, if you want a triangle to measure 10 in. deep (to the point), you will have to set on sufficient threads to a holding cord to measure 20 in. across.

Work a practice sample to determine the number of set-on threads needed to give 1 in. measurement on the holding cord. If you find 2 threads set on equal 1 in., then you will require a total of 40 altogether to give 20 in. across (80 working ends). The central 2 threads should be cut to the length of 80 in. each (8 times 10), and then 19 threads set on either side of the central threads, decreasing the length of each thread by 4 in. every time so the outer threads eventually will measure only 4 in. — but as they will only be used to work one flat knot each and one double half hitch this should be sufficient.

*Student's notebook recording design ideas and knotting patterns.*

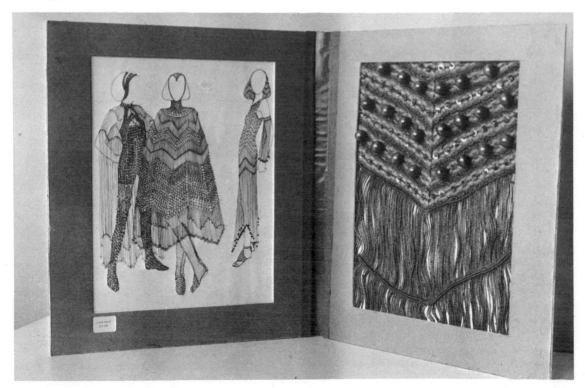

### A typical entry in a record book

The following entry, taken from my note-book should help to show you the sort of information it is worth recording.

**Project.** Belt mounted on rings.

**Yarn.** Multi-coloured synthetic cord.

**Pattern.** Sinnets of 3 flat knots, linked by single flat knots, in the alternate pattern.

**Mounting.** Reversed double half hitch.

**Finishing.** Double half hitches; 2-end flat knots at the back of work.

**Quantity of yarn used.** 20 yd., cut into 6 equal lengths.

**Remarks.** Knots tend to slip because of nature of yarn, but if pinned securely and each row tightened by the subsequent one, effect is pleasing, and work grows rapidly.

**Important.** Not nearly enough yarn bought – another 7 yd. would have been needed to produce belt of a wearable size. As it is it might just fit a very slim toddler! On the whole, however, it was money wasted. Remember for next time.

A note should also be made of where you purchased the yarn, its price, and other colours available. If possible, a rough sketch of the item made should be shown, and an actual sample of the yarn attached.

## MEASURING AND CUTTING CORDS

The time spent on calculating cord lengths, measuring, cutting and setting on can often – especially with an ambitious project – take longer than the actual knotting!

And measuring out and cutting cord lengths can be a mammoth task in itself. But this stage of initial preparation, like cutting out pattern pieces in dressmaking, or casting on stitches in knitting, although indeed tedious compared with the exciting business of creating a design, be it by sewing, knitting or knotting, is very important, and worth taking trouble to do properly. Fortunately, there are ways to make the task a little easier.

With small and moderately sized designs, the problem is not too great. Simply measure off one end of yarn accurately against a metal rule or tape measure, then use this end as a guide to cut the other lengths. But this method is not so satisfactory for bigger projects where a vast number of yarn ends are required.

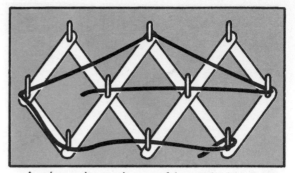

Again various pieces of household equipment and furniture can be put to good use to assist you. If you are lucky enough to have a weaver's warping board, or can beg, buy or borrow one this is an ideal measuring guide. Cut the first cord to the required length, measuring it against a rule or tape measure. Then wind one end on to a peg on the warping board, and take it round sufficient pegs almost to its end, and loop it over the nearest peg. Subsequent cords are then measured round the same 'course'.

Any sort of expanding pegboard can be used in a similar way – a clothes drier, for instance, or a coat rack.

Even if the actual rack is quite small, cords can be criss-crossed from one side of the rack to the other until the full extent of their length has been used up. Once the 'route' has been established, providing all future cords are taken across the same route they will be the required length.

Clamps of any kind make good measuring devices too. Attach clamps to a table surface, or to a workbench, piece of wood or stiff card, spacing them apart so distance equals length of cords required, then simply wind yarn from one clamp to the other.

Whichever method you use it simplifies and speeds the process if you wind ten cords at a time, and then tie a loop of cord or rubber band round each group.

If you have no warping board or clamps, try any of the following makeshift but reasonably satisfactory methods: place two chairs back to back the required distance apart, and wind the yarn round a knob or other protuberance of the chair; if two adjacent or opposite doors happen to have their handles the required distance apart, yarn can be wound round them (make sure first no one is in either of the rooms!) – yarn can be cut through at one fold only,

leaving the ends ready doubled for mounting (distance of door knobs apart should then be equal to *half* the total length of cord required).

Wedge wooden spoons in adjacent drawers, at the appropriate distance apart. Wind yarn round the spoon handles — again you only need to cut through at one fold. For cords of more manageable length, wind yarn round an oblong of strong cardboard cut to the required length.

## WORKING WITH LONG ENDS

If joining is to be avoided in mid-work, then large items will inevitably mean you have to work with excessively long cords, and this presents problems in itself. Lengthy ends can get tangled with each other, and are difficult to sort out and keep in order while knotting — in fact, the tying of a single knot becomes a complex undertaking.

Long ends therefore have to be controlled in some way, and reduced to manageable size, and there are several ways of doing this. Again, it is worth taking time and trouble when you set on threads to organise them so knotting can proceed swiftly and smoothly.

If you are working a pattern which involves several repeats of the same motif, first group the cords into the number required per motif, and either tie the bundles loosely together with an overhand knot, or hold together with a rubber band. Individual ends can then be 'shortened' by any of the methods listed below. Whichever method you choose it is important that the

yarn should be able to slip easily through as you work, without having to stop constantly to untie and reassemble cord ends.

### Butterflies

These may be secured with rubber bands, or self tied. To secure with a rubber band, begin winding ends from about 18 in. from knotting. Wind yarn round fingers to the end of the length, then slip a rubber band round bundle. Yarn should feed out as you work, providing the rubber band is not too tight.

For a self-tied butterfly, wind as before, finish butterfly with a few turns of cord round centre of bundle and tie end to cord coming from the knotting with a double half hitch.

### Bobbins

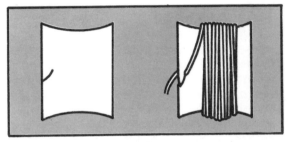

**Card or wood bobbins.** Cut card or thin wood into small oblongs, approximately 2 in. by 1 in. Wind each cord round a separate bobbin, starting from the end of the yarn this time; stop winding about 18 in. from knotting. A small slit cut in the side of the bobbin will allow yarn to be slotted in and prevent it unwinding too quickly. Providing the slot is not too tight, yarn should feed out as required.

**Hand bobbin.** Starting at end of yarn, wind in loose circles to within about 18 in. of knotting, then loop cord end round the wound circles and tie with a double half hitch to cord coming from knotting.

## Looped chain

This is my favourite method of coping with long ends, as sometimes bobbins or butterflies can be awkward to take through knots. Start at end of yarn and make a loop. Make another loop just beyond this and pull second loop through first. Draw tight. Make a third loop, and pull it through the second one. Draw tight. Continue in this way making a continuous looped chain. The excessive length of each cord will quickly be shortened and the yarn feeds out extremely easily as you work.

## Double half hitch method

If cords are not excessively long they can be shortened to a manageable length simply by folding cord back on itself and securing with a double half hitch. Slide the double half hitch along as work progresses. When the knot reaches the end of the doubled length of cord, it will not slide off by itself, but will have to be untied. Take care not to forget to do this – the knot can easily get worked into the main knotting without noticing and will cause an ugly irregularity in the pattern.

## JOINING IN NEW ENDS

Ideally and with accurate pre-planning sufficient lengths of yarn should be cut before you begin work to take you right through to the completion of knotting. Unfortunately such a perfect state of affairs seldom exists and yarns run out at the most awkward moments in a design.

Several convenient methods of joining in new cords are explained in the chapter dealing with working in the round (page 96) and also in the chapter on shaping (page 118), but yarns – being contrary and apparently taking on lives of their own – will run out where none of the convenient methods, such as adding with cording, or looping into an alternate flat knot pattern, can be used.

In such situations, other less satisfactory

methods have to be used, and the following suggestions should provide an answer for most purposes. If you see a yarn is running short it is usually better not to wait until the last possible moment before adding a new length, but to add a new cord wherever the most convenient situation occurs – even if this does mean wasting a few precious inches of yarn.

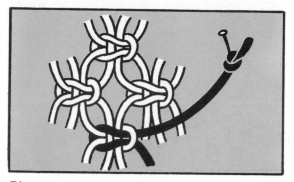

Pin new cord to working surface through overhand knot, and introduce to work where old cord has finished, bringing it through from back of knotting to the front. When work is complete untie overhand knot and tie the loose ends from the old cord and the new one together on the wrong side of knotting, using either a 2-end flat knot or a weaver's knot.

To tie a weaver's knot, lay cords at right angles to each other, bring cord 1 up and over cord 2, behind itself from left to right, and down over cord 2. Now bring cord 2 from right to left over cord 1, and through loop formed by it. Draw knot tight.

If you find core ends are much longer than knotting ends in a flat knot pattern, it is sometimes possible to switch them so you continue knotting using the core ends as knotting cords, and the previous knotting cords become the central core.

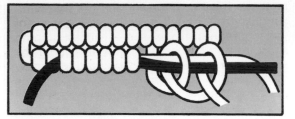

In a row of cording, a new cord can be over-lapped with the old one, and both worked over together for a few knots. Pull loose ends of both cords to reverse of work and darn them neatly in.

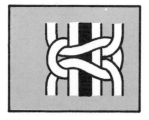

When working flat knots a new cord can be introduced by adding to central core with the old end, and again working over the combined thickness for a short distance. Pull loose ends to back of work, and darn them in afterwards.

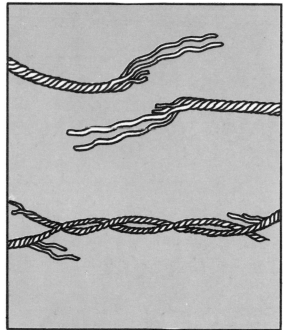

**Splicing.** With thick yarns splicing is the only adequate answer for joining in a new cord. Working over a double thickness would create too much bulk. A simple splice is achieved by unravelling the end of the old cord and the beginning of new cord for a few inches, and cutting away a few strands of each. Twist the two ends together so they are equal to one thickness of the basic yarn and work this into the pattern. Any loose ends can be trimmed away later or darned into the reverse of work. A spot of glue added to the splice will keep it firmly in place.

This is a simple splice which will serve most straightforward joining purposes. It is worth however looking through sailors' knotting manuals to find more elaborate splices, for a judiciously chosen and carefully worked splice can give a neat and extremely pro-fessional finish to your knotting.

### WHEN YOU MAKE A MISTAKE...

Alas, none of us is perfect, and of course sooner or later you will make a mistake in your knotting. Just a brief interruption in mid-knot, like the telephone ringing, the baby crying, or a neighbour calling, can lead to your missing out a vital step or doing one step twice...Sometimes the irregularity does not become apparent until a good chunk more of the pattern has been worked.

There is only one solution: you must undo the knots back to this point and start again. If the mistake occurs in a flat knot sinnet, simply take hold of the central core cords from the top and pull them right out of the sinnets. The remaining knots are then quick to untie.

If the mistake occurs in cording, take hold of the leader and give a sharp tug to pull it out — hey presto, the whole row of cording will be undone. Vertical or diagonal cording can be ripped out in the same way, by pulling out the leader cord in each case.

# Simple shaping

Until now most of the samplers given, other than in-the-round designs, have been basically oblong forms with any shaping created by gathering ends at the bottom into tassels or other collecting knots.

It is however possible to achieve fairly intricate shaping for garments and other articles where a regular outline is not wanted. In knitting and crochet, shaping is usually achieved by adding or subtracting stitches. With macramé however other methods are available.

*19th century edging, in imitation of Genoese macramé lace, with shaped cording motifs.*

Cords can be reduced by working them together in multiple end knots, also by merely slackening the knots or tightening them as required shaping can be achieved.

A holding cord can be curved into a desired shape, and threads set on to this, thus creating a shaped beginning.

## METHODS

Simple shaping to a point (for a belt end, for instance) can be achieved in various ways. For a flat knot pattern alone there are three possible methods:

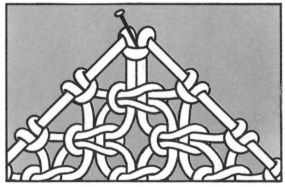

**Method 1.** Set required number of threads on to a holding cord with reversed double half hitches (total of threads should equal an odd number). Pin at central point to working surface, then allow holding cord to fall to an inverted 'V' on either side of the pin. Work in alternate flat knot pattern, knotting cords 6 and 9 over 7 and 8 in the first row.
**2nd row:** knot 4 and 7 over 5 and 6; knot 8 and 11 over 9 and 10.
**3rd row:** knot 2 and 5 over 3 and 4; 6 and 9 over 7 and 8; 10 and 13 over 11 and 12.
Continue in the alternate flat knot pattern.

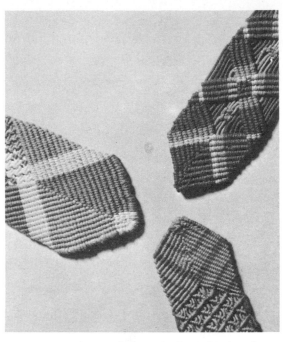

Cording can be used to work shaped belt points.

**Method 3.** Cut 2 lengths of yarn, and tie a flat knot with them, as for the beginning of any flat knot picot edging (see page 102). Pin to working surface and working in alternate flat knot pattern, add a doubled thread to either side of first flat knot, so 2nd row will have 2 knots; continue to add cords in this way, so 3rd row will have 3 knots; 4th row will have 4 knots — and so on to the depth required (see diagram at bottom of previous column).

In all these methods the shaped point may be divided from the rest of work with a row of horizontal cording, if wished.

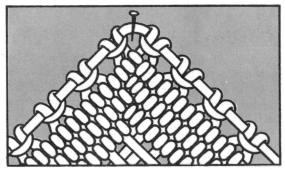

**Shaping with cording.** Mount cords and pin them at the central point as for Method 1 or 2 of flat knot shaping, then work 3 rows of diagonal cording from the pin down either side. Use the cords at centre of work as leaders for each row.

An alternative method of shaping to a point with cording can be seen on the hairband on page 146. This is worked as follows: set 2 threads on to a holding cord (or tie in a flat knot picot). Lay a leader across and work cording over it with each of the 4 ends.

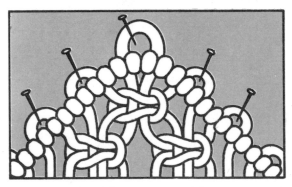

**Method 2.** Mount an odd number of threads with simple picot edging (small picots only) to a holding cord. Pin at central point as for Method 1, and work in alternate flat knot pattern in the same way.

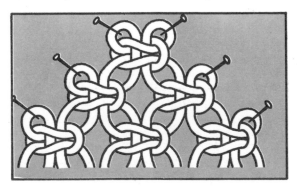

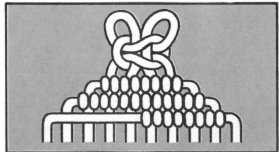

At the end of the row fold down both ends of the leader to become knotting cords.

Introduce another leader and knot all 6 ends over it. At the end of the row both ends of this leader become knotting cords for subsequent row.

Introduce another leader and knot the 8 cords over it. Continue in this way until required width of knotting is achieved.

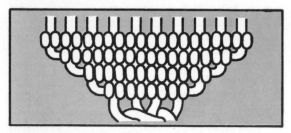

To decrease graduated cording, simply stop knotting one cord from the end on each succeeding row. Ends can be concealed at the back or woven into row ends afterwards.

## SHAPING TO A POINT (DECREASING METHOD)

A very simple and speedy method of decreasing to a point to produce a triangular shape can be worked in the alternate flat knot pattern. The size of the triangle is governed by the number of set-on threads (see note on page 113). A very tiny triangle can be produced using only a few cords; whereas with a suitable number of cords, big items such as shawls can be made (see pattern on page 155).

Set on threads in multiples of 4 to a holding cord. Work in the alternate flat knot pattern, dropping 2 ends from each side of the row on every row until you reach the point of triangle (i.e. last row will have only one knot in it). Diagonal cording can be worked down sides of triangle to give a firm edging and if holding cord has been left long enough at either side, these lengths may be leaders.

## GENERAL SHAPING

Decreasing the width of a piece can easily be achieved by ceasing to knot cords. The outline of the shape can then be emphasised with a row of cording, if wished, and the ends either left to hang in a fringe or trimmed, turned to the back of work, and enclosed in a seam binding or fabric lining. Cords can be added to increase width of

work by looping on to the loops of worked knots (see sketches below), or by introducing in cording, either by mounting with double half hitches, or by using as a leader and then becoming a knotting cord in subsequent rows.

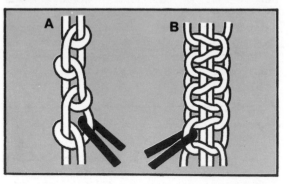

Diagram A shows how to loop a new cord into an alternate half hitch chain; diagram B shows how to loop a new cord into a flat knot sinnet; the 2nd diagram on page 99 shows how to loop in 2 new cords in an alternate flat knot pattern.

Before beginning work on a shaped design, draw the outline on your working surface, then knot over this shape, stopping knotting where required in order to achieve curves and other shaping refinements. When extra width is required, add cords by whatever method seems appropriate.

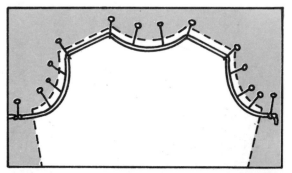

Before embarking on an ambitious project, practise working over an old dressmaking paper pattern – the simpler the shape the better. A classic sun top, for instance, would be a good design to start with. Pin paper pattern to your working surface and follow its outline as closely as possible. A holding cord pinned round shoulder line, neckline and armholes gives a good basis on which to work. Set on threads at shoulders, and work down, adding new cords as required to reach armhole and neckline holding cords.

Link working cords to these holding cords with double half hitches, or reversed double half hitches, or flat knots — whatever suits the pattern best. If the holding cord turns a definite corner (e.g. at under-arm point) then add new cords by setting them directly on to holding cord then working them into main pattern (see fringed waistcoat, page 166).

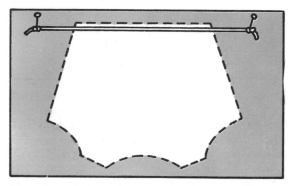

If preferred, knotting can begin at the lower edge of a garment, and work towards the top. In this case a holding cord would be pinned right round lower edge and threads set on to this. Knotting would stop and start as required to achieve neckline and armhole shaping, with cording worked round the shaped edges to give them firmness.

## ANGLING TECHNIQUE

This technique can be used to produce sharp points in your work, and when working in

two or more colours of yarn, to give an attractive colour pattern. It is worked in vertical and horizontal cording as follows:

For practice sampler, set on 4 threads in colour A, 4 threads in colour B. Using cord 1 as leader, work a complete row of horizontal cording from left to right. Leave leader extended to the right of work, and work a second row of cording from left to right over cord 2. End row where previous row finished.

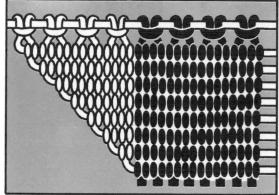

Now use cord 3 as a leader and work another row of cording from left to right to finish beneath previous 2 rows. Continue in this way, always using the cord on the far left as leader and finishing each row at the same point beneath the previous ones, until all the cords in colour A have been used as leaders.

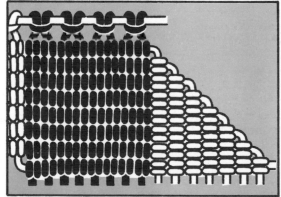

With the original cord 1 as leader, work vertical cording with cords 2, 3, 4, 5, 6, 7 and 8, then use cord 2 as leader and work vertical cording with cords 3, 4, 5, 6, 7 and 8. Continue in this way until vertical cording is worked with cord 7.

At this point the design may continue further to the right in another sequence of colour by using cord 9 as leader and working horizontal cording across the row. Continue as before working a section of horizontal cording with leaders from colour B, then vertical cording on these colour B cords.

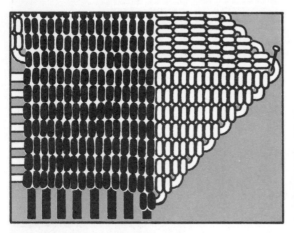

If it is wished to bring work back to a point on the left-hand side, merely reverse the direction of cord 8 round a pin, to form a leader for horizontal cording from right to left. Continue as before, but this time leaders for horizontal cording will be taken one at a time from the right-hand side of work, in colour A.

When each colour A cord has been used as leader, then vertical cording is continued on left-hand side of work in colour A. The combination of different cording directions and the interplay of colours makes this pattern a particularly pleasing and attractive one.

If wished, the zig-zag pattern can be worked in one colour only, sufficient textural interest being provided by the change of cording direction.

On the other hand, a similar zig-zag shape can be achieved by working in horizontal cording throughout. Begin working from left to right, using cord on the far left as leader for each successive row. In this case as each leader is taken to the right, it becomes a knotting cord in the subsequent row. When it is wished to bring work back to the left, the outer right-hand cord is reversed round a pin to become leader, and cording continues from right to left. The cord on the far right

becomes leader for each successive row.

Another interesting two-colour braid (see illustration below) can be worked as follows: set on 2 groups of threads, one group in colour A, one in colour B, to the same holding cord. Now work each group independently in the horizontal zig-zag pattern as described above. The first point of the zig-zag should be knotted from right to left for group A cords; from left to right for group B cords. At a chosen point combine all the cords with a single row of horizontal cording.

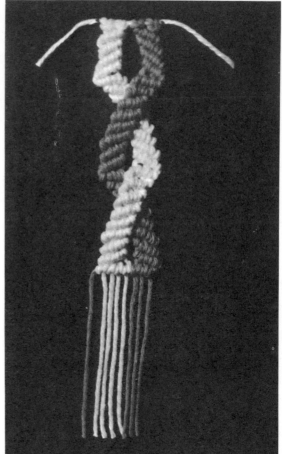

## TURNING CORNERS

As a general rule, cording is the most useful technique for working corners. Providing leaders extend from work at suitable points it is a simple matter to continue knotting in any direction (and pattern) wished, or new cords can be set on to the leaders. Careful planning is necessary when turning corners, or for any other form of complex shaping in order to have cords hanging exactly where they are needed.

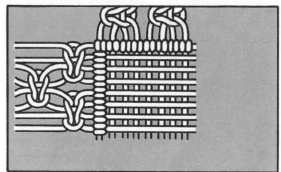

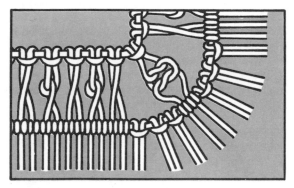

Working a corner by holding cord method: a holding cord is pinned to working surface to form a corner, and threads set on and worked in chosen knotting pattern for a few inches. When new cords are required to fill in the corner area, work a row of cording and add new cords at the corner with double half hitches over the leader. Continue in pattern. When knotting is complete, ends may be trimmed to give a sharp corner, or left in a curve if preferred.

Two separate strips of knotting may also be combined at a corner (to form a border, for instance, for a tablecloth, or cushion cover). Work each strip independently in chosen knotting pattern. When corner is reached, lay the strips at right angles to each other, so their working cords criss-cross. Join to each other with rows of cording (see diagram, above).

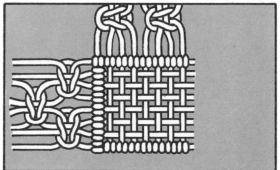

Centre of square may be filled in with a continuation of the pattern, or left as floating unworked cords. Cording should be worked at outside edge to 'contain' the corner.

If it is wished to join four strips into a complete border, threads for each strip should be set on to a holding cord singly by double half hitches and enough length of threads left to form the corner when combined with another strip.

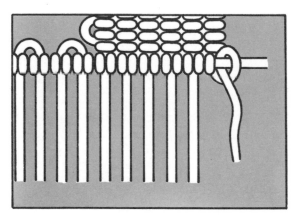

Another way to work a corner, this time with solid cording. Work cording to required depth, using new leaders every 2 rows. Turn work on its side so leaders become working cords. Lay new leader across work, as shown in diagram. Set new cords on to it with double half hitches, and work cording right across row.

# Working with other materials

## BEADS AND BUTTONS

Although macramé can be most happily combined with all sorts of materials one of the simplest and most effective methods of adding interest to your work is to incorporate beads or buttons with the knots. The contrast between solid bead and textured knotting is particularly pleasing.

Any shape or form of beads may be used — china, wooden, plastic, metal — to suit the knotting design. If the holes are not big enough for the yarn to go through, then their size can usually be increased by gentle drilling. Similarly if it is wished to attach other, less conventional, decorative items such as sea shells (see headband on page 127), acorns or even old coins to your work, simply drill holes at the point where you wish to attach the items.

Fascinating jewellery can be created by combining various macramé braids with beads and other items. Buttons with shanks at the back can be used too, so can small lengths of plastic or metal tubing, and beads from a child's abacus.

Have a search through your button box — or a leisurely browse in a haberdashery department or craft shop — you're bound to find some fascinating items to use to enhance your knotting.

It is possible nowadays to buy a preparation from which to make your own ceramic beads. It is very easy to use and hardens without kiln firing. Mould the clay round any suitable shaped object to give a hole large enough to slide on to your macramé yarn.

Beads can be introduced wherever you want them, to form a single focal point in a pattern, or used in a repeated motif. Just slide the bead on to the end of yarn and up into place in the knotting. Overhand knots tied either side of the bead will keep it in position but of course other knots can be used if preferred.

Beads are normally added to core ends but can be added to knotting cords if wished. If you are adding beads to a flat knot sinnet then slip bead on to centre core cords, bring outer cords fairly tightly round sides of bead and tie next flat knot immediately below bead to keep it securely in position.

If it is difficult to thread beads on to yarn, sometimes dipping the yarn end in colourless nail varnish and allowing it to dry will make it sufficiently rigid to slip easily through the bead. The varnished end can be cut away afterwards.

If a particular bead is exactly the one you want for a project and it is quite impossible either to thread it on to your yarn, or to widen the hole in any way, then wire the bead on to the yarn at the appropriate place in your work with fine fuse wire, keeping wire hidden at back of knotting.

To thread beads on to soft threads, such as embroidery silks, knitting yarns and rug wool: first calculate how many beads you will require, and decide where you want them

An impressive three-dimensional knotted sculpture showing how macramè can be used as a modern art form. Continuous solid cording is worked in thick ropes to create fascinating spirals of colòur.

to appear and on which cords, then count out the correct total number of beads required for each cord. Cut a length of nylon thread long enough to take all the beads, with a good 6 in. over. Tie an overhand knot at one end, thread the other on to a needle fine enough to go through the beads. String beads on to nylon.

Remove needle and tie end of nylon around one of your working cords. It is important to do it this way, and not to tie macramé yarn round nylon.

Very carefully slide the beads over the knot and so on to the yarn, taking care not to break the nylon. When the required number of beads are on the cord, remove nylon. Tie an overhand knot at the end of cord to stop beads falling off. Repeat threading process for each cord in turn. When knotting begins, the beads are pushed up into your pattern as and when required.

Many of the designs shown throughout this book use bead decoration in some form or another, and these should help to give some ideas for making the best use of the combination. Look particularly at the sampler on page 128 — this example demonstrates a most interesting and attractive blend of different yarns (dishcloth cotton and raffia) with wooden and china beads.

Beads may be functional as well as decorative as they can be threaded on to cord ends, and secured with overhand knots to give a firm finish to your knotting. They can also be added to the ends of leader cords to form a side decoration (see border 2, page 51).

## KNITTING AND CROCHET

Because macramé can be worked in such a diversity of yarns, a careful choice of knotting pattern and yarn can make the technique compatible with virtually any other material.

Added in a fringe to a crochet or knitted item, for instance, and worked in the same yarn, it is almost impossible to tell where one craft form ends and the other begins!

When making a garment in macramé, instead of setting on threads to holding

*White bikini — see pattern section, page 164.*

*Above: headband made from a flat knot braid, with beads, sea shells, and other ornaments. Below: simply worked cravat in wool with panels of beads and knots.*

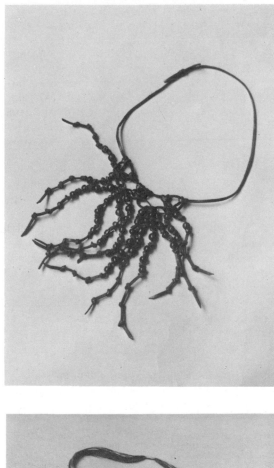

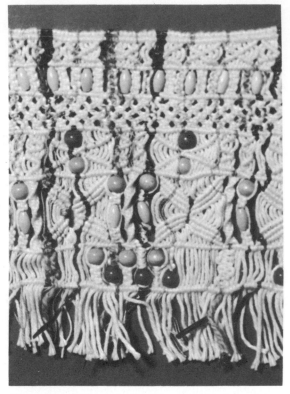

*Top left: necklace worked in green leather with flat knots and green glass beads. Above: sampler using dishcloth cotton, raffia and wooden beads. Left: necklaces in wool and metal threads.*

cords or macramé braids, work a long crochet chain, and pin this to the outline of pattern, then set on threads to the loops of the crochet chain. This gives a firm and attractive edging to the design.

## FABRICS

Both soft furnishings and fashion outfits can benefit from the judicious use of macramé decoration. A dress in a plain fabric, for instance, can be taken into couture class by adding macramé cuffs, collar or hem edge — or even a knotted midriff insert.

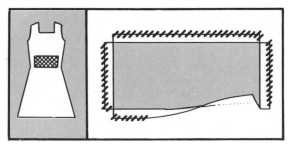

**To make a dress with macramé midriff**, choose a simple classic style of dress, similar to the one sketched, below left. Decide the depth of macramé insert you wish to make — either one of the two borders shown on pages 50 and 51 would be suitable.

Trim away this area on the paper pattern, but leave a ½-in. seam allowance all round. Make up dress in the usual way, then fold in seam allowance all round insert area, and hemstitch in place.

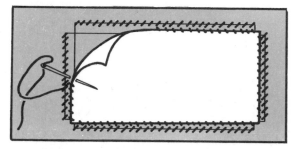

Work macramé border in a yarn to match or contrast with dress fabric, and sew insert to dress with neat overcasting stitches.

Alternatively threads can be set directly on to the fabric, and the knotting worked *in situ*. The various methods of setting threads on to fabric are on page 130.

It is possible to set threads on to any fabric but non-fraying fabrics such as felt, canvas and PVC, where no hemming is required, are particularly suitable. Other fabrics should have raw edges turned in and hemstitched before setting on macramé threads, otherwise the pull of the knotting could fray out the fabric.

Leather, suede and similar materials should have holes punched along their edges for threads to be set on. See, for example, the suede bag on right. Oddments of blue suede were combined with macramé braids and an insert worked in blue linen twine to produce a most original and attractive bag. Holes were punched in the suede along top and bottom of main panel at two different levels so threads could be set on in a decorative pattern. Cords were also threaded through holes down sides of panel at each end of every row of knotting.

The bag shown on back cover was also made from offcuts of suede, combined with a macramé panel worked in synthetic tubular cord. The panel was knotted separately and machine stitched to the front of bag when complete.

Yet another way of combining fabric and macramé for a bag is on page 80. Here the basic fabric bag in cyclamen pink was first made with fabric mounted directly on to a handbag frame. Then a separate outer patterned covering was knotted in black synthetic tubular cord, and this stitched to top of fabric just below the frame. A lining and a metal chain handle completed the design.

The glove puppet pictured on page 108 shows a delightful and cleverly designed combination of many different needlework techniques: dressmaking, patchwork, beading, plaiting, toy making — with macramé used as a trimming right round the edge of the yoked cape. Small rings and beads are incorporated into the knotting.

### FRINGES

Threads for fringes may be set on by pulling cords through with a crochet hook, or each cut end can be threaded on to a large-eyed

*Suede bucket bag with macramé braid trimmings, and inset patterned panel in matching twine.*

129

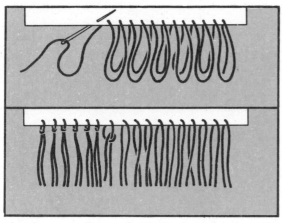

darning needle, and stitched to fabric with one small horizontal stitch then the ends of thread taken through the loop of stitch and pulled down so it resembles a reversed double half hitch setting-on. Alternatively, for a more decorative effect, the threads may be stitched on with a small vertical stitch, or a criss-cross stitch.

In order not to have to thread and unthread the needle continually, measure out length of yarn required for entire fringe, and thread on to a large-eyed darning needle. Working from right to left, bring needle through fabric edge, from the wrong side to the right side. Continue to take stitches in a similar way across fabric, leaving big loops to the depth of fringe required between stitches.

When all the yarn has been 'stitched' on, cut loops, and tie each pair of ends in an overhand knot, just below fabric edge.

A fringe can be knotted separately and sewn to a fabric afterwards either with neat hemstitching, or with decorative embroidery stitches. Any type of macramé braid too can be added to fabrics in this way. Fringed rugs are attractive — set cords for fringe directly on to the rug backing. Again, a crochet hook will make the job much easier.

### Two fringes to make

Suitable for household items, such as blinds, curtains, table mats, chair covers and other similar items.

### Fringe 1

Set directly on to fabric edge.
**YARN.** Thin nylon cord.
**MEASUREMENT.** Finished fringe measures approximately 8 in. deep (including tassel).
**PREPARATION.** To work section of fringe shown, cut 10 threads, each 5 ft. long. Double them and set them directly on to fabric edge by any of the methods explained on page 130.
You now have 20 working ends.
**Note.** If a greater area of fringing is required then set on more cords in any multiple of 4.
**TO MAKE.** Work 3 rows of triple knots (flat knot followed by a half knot) in the alternate sequence.
**Next row:** leave first 2 cords unworked; work 2 banister bars (sinnets of half knots), with 8 knots in each bar — allow the sinnet to twist round after the 4th half knot. Leave last 2 cords unworked.
Work 3 rows of triple knots in the alternate sequence.

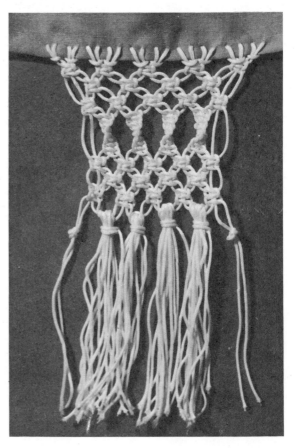

**TO FINISH.** Make a plain tassel, 5 in. deep, below every flat knot in the last row (see page 85).

### Fringe 2

Made separately, and attached when complete to fabric edge
**YARN.** Synthetic tubular cord in 2 colours (dark and light).
**MEASUREMENT.** Finished fringe measures approximately 10 in. deep.
**PREPARATION.** Cut 12 threads, each 8 ft., 6 in each colour. Double them and set them with reversed double half hitches on to a holding cord about 12 in. long (24 working ends). Set on cords so one dark colour is at each end, then arrange 2 light, 2 dark, alternately between.

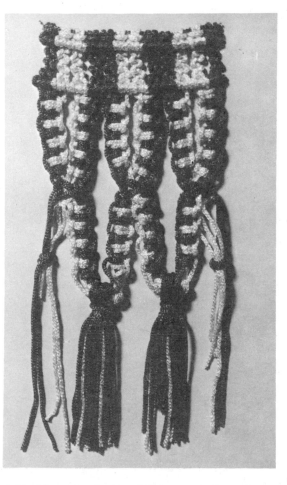

**Note.** If a greater area of fringing is required then set on more cords in any multiple of 8.
**TO MAKE.** Attach a separate leader approximately 12 in. long to left-hand side of work, and work a row of horizontal cording across all cords.
Work single alternate half hitch chains with each pair of cords, tying 6 knots in each chain (3 from each side).
Attach a separate leader approximately 12 in. long to left-hand side of work, and work a row of horizontal cording across all cords.
Divide cords into groups of 4. Work a tatted bar on each group (reversed double half hitches worked alternately from left and right over a central knot-bearing core) to a depth of 2 in.
Now link each pair of tatted bars by tying a multi-end flat knot: 2 outer pairs of knotting cords, 4 central knot-bearing core cords.
Leave first 4 cords unworked, then work 4

tatted bars to depth of 2 in., as before; leave final 4 cords unworked.
**TO FINISH.** Link the 2 pairs of tatted bars by making a plain tassel over them 4 in. deep, as explained on page 85.

# The importance of design

## SPECIAL EFFECTS

As with any other craft form there are certain tricks of the trade which are simple to do yet will give an extra 'fillip' to your work. Here are just a few ideas — you will probably invent many more yourself.

### Reverse knotting

This is not a specially difficult form of knotting, but merely the effect of using the wrong side of cording on the right side of work. All forms of the flat knot — in the alternate pattern, in Solomon's bars, and in waved bars — look exactly the same from either side but cording, and also Genoese bars and some of the fancy knots (including the true lover's knot) give a completely different pattern effect on the right and wrong sides.

Turn some of your cording samplers to the wrong side and have a look! This effect can be used on its own, or can be combined with regular cording for a pleasing textural contrast. Whenever you wish to use reverse cording, simply turn the work to the wrong side and continue to knot from there. Turn back to the right side when you want regular cording.

The belts shown above, right, use reverse cording in their knotting patterns. Try the following simple cording sampler just to get the idea of the technique.

*Unusual use of macramé — a veil knotted in nylon cord. Threads were set on with simple picots round top edge, and shaped panels of flat knots worked round sides and back of head.*

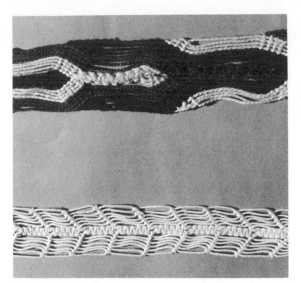

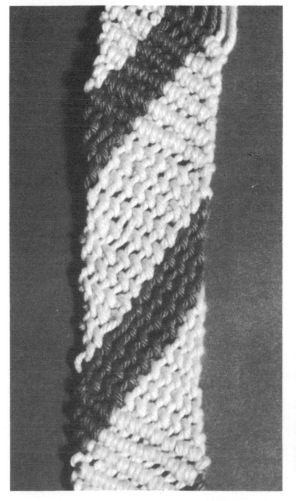

*Above: belts using reverse cording pattern.*
*Below: reverse cording sampler.*

### Reverse cording sampler

**YARN.** Crochet cotton in three contrasting colours.

**MEASUREMENT.** Finished sampler measures approximately 10 in. by 2 in.

**PREPARATION.** Cut threads each 9 ft. long — 2 in colour A, 2 in colour B, 2 in colour C. Double them and set them on to a holding cord about 6 in. long with simple picot edging: 4 working ends in colour A, 4 working ends in colour B, 4 working ends in colour C.

**TO MAKE.** Work 12 rows of diagonal cording slanting to the right, using the cord on the far left as leader for each row.

Now unpin work from working base, turn it over and continue knotting on wrong side thus:

Work 12 rows of diagonal cording slanting to the left, using the cord on the far right as leader for each row.

Unpin work and turn to right side again.

Work 12 rows of diagonal cording slanting to the right, using the cord on the far left as leader for each row.

Work 1 row of horizontal cording from right to left, using cord on far right as leader.

**TO FINISH.** Trim ends to give fringe.

### Plaiting

Almost everyone knows how to plait, for it is one of the things we usually learn to do in early childhood. Yet this simple technique is an adjunct of macramé and can be used to complement knotting patterns: use plaiting to give a firm edging; as an alternative to a fringe; or incorporated in knotting pattern.

Divide cords into groups of three and form plaited sinnets. They can then be combined in a pattern with flat knot sinnets or used on their own between bands of cording.

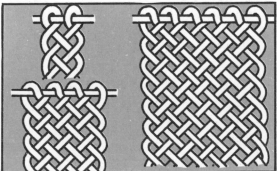

It is not always necessary to plait with the conventional three strands — the diagrams on previous page show how plaiting can be done with four, eight and twelve strands.

## Criss-cross weaving

Another pleasing effect is easily achieved by weaving cords in a criss-cross fashion over each other. This technique can be used in areas of unworked cords, with a few of them arranged in a simple criss-cross, or within cording motifs, woven closely over and under each other. Sinnets may also be criss-crossed over each other — this device is used on the bag on page 148 to create a textural pattern within an over-all alternate flat knot pattern.

If working criss-crosses within a diamond pattern of cording, the top two sides of the diamond are knotted first then the criss-cross weaving is worked (a crochet hook is useful here for pulling cords under and over each other) followed by the final two rows of cording.

Criss-crosses can be worked on single, double, triple or any grouping of cords. If sinnets are knotted in different colours, then criss-crossed, a checked pattern is created.

*Sculptured head uses flat knot loops to simulate hair.*

## Loops

The formation of any sort of looped motif is particularly attractive on three-dimensional work. These loops may be from single or multiple cords, or can be formed with flat knot sinnets. The chess set on page 72, the sculptured head mask above, and the light pull below all demonstrate the flat knot loop.

*Belts using criss-cross patterns of sinnets.*

*Light pull also demonstrates flat knot loops.*

**Flat knot loop.** A flat knot sinnet is worked at the point where the loop is required to a sufficient length for depth of loop then caught back into the main work with the next row of flat knots or cording. The yarn can be strengthened with wire if it is not rigid enough to hold shape of loop. This forms an open-ended loop which is quite different from the solid, close-textured bead knot.

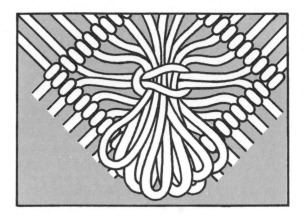

**Single cord loops.** These are effective when worked at the central point of a motif where several cords meet. Only the two outer cords will be used as knotting cords – the others are all formed into deep loops, and a flat knot tied round them with the outer cords.

### Combination of different yarns

By combining apparently incompatible yarns – e.g. raffia and rug wool; fine knitting cotton and plastic-coated twine – fascinating effects can be achieved. Obviously with any such experimenting, it is essential to practise small samplers in the combination first: the effect might be totally unacceptable – or, on the other hand, totally dramatic! You won't know until you try.

When working with combinations of yarn it saves time and trouble in the long run to wind the yarns together and then treat the combined strands as one for the purpose of setting on and knotting.

Begin experimenting by selecting one of the simple samplers from earlier in the book, and make it up in any of the yarn combinations given above. Compare it to your original one-yarn samplers . . . see the difference?

Another interesting and pretty effect can be achieved by knotting with ribbon – the narrow variety sold to thread through baby garments is the most successful. Pretty ribbon braids can be worked and used to trim fashion garments.

## PLANNING YOUR OWN PATTERNS

By now your mind should be teeming with ideas for new projects. For macramé, more than almost any other craft form, seems to inspire individuality and originality of design, even with people who have never considered themselves to be creative designers before. And provided knotting is kept regular and even, it is almost impossible not to produce a design which is pleasing to the eye.

As you become more macramé-minded, you will begin to look at everything around you with a view to adapting it to a macramé pattern. All sorts of everyday objects will inspire you – an ornate gate or fence, for example, will offer a pattern of curves and decorative motifs which can easily be translated into knotting; so too can a tree, a flower, a pot plant – even a particular arrangement of tiles on a roof, or intertwined telegraph wires.

Apart from anything else it is good to start looking at the world with a fresh eye. You will be surprised, for instance, how decorative the roofs of buildings are, and no doubt a little ashamed to realise you have never really looked at them before.

In the textile field, both knitting and crochet work are extremely easy to adapt into macramé. If you want to make a particular fashion garment, and are uncertain how to begin, have a look through the crochet and knitting patterns in any magazine, and select one which most closely resembles the item you wish to make. It is usually a comparatively simple matter to translate the pattern into macramé.

Solid horizontal areas can be worked in cording; open-work areas in flat knot sinnets, or alternate flat knots; 'chunky' parts of the design in alternate half hitch chains. The sampler scarf on page 157 was based on a crochet pattern, so also was the fringed waistcoat on page 166.

One word of warning: the search for macramé inspiration can lead to embarrassing situations! I frequently while away a train or bus journey by scrutinising the clothing patterns around me. One day I became enthralled by a particularly exciting pattern worn by a fellow traveller, and I leaned ever closer to get a clearer view. Only the curious and very suspicious glance from the wearer brought me to my senses in time – and I

135

recalled the pattern was attached to a person!

Many other craft forms can spark off ideas too — canvas work, tapestry (Cavandoli work can give an almost exact replica), embroidery, basket weaving — and so on.

Traditional knitting patterns can also be emulated — Aran patterns, for example, adapt easily. The multi-coloured table mat on page 158, worked entirely in diagonal cording, shows a replica of a woven plaid pattern.

### Noting down ideas

Before embarking on a project you've designed yourself, it is best to jot down all your ideas on paper. It is surprising how easily a brilliant idea can get forgotten — even by the following day — when your mind has had to cope in the interim with a day's work, compiling shopping lists, planning household menus — and other such menial pursuits.

If your thoughts are all recorded in your notebook then there is no danger of an idea ever being overlooked or passed by.

Rough sketches of possible items to make help too, with notes about yarns to use, and knots to work.

### Finally, a word about samplers...

If you have worked your way steadily step by step through every lesson in this book you should by now have a pile of fascinating knotted samplers.

A sampler is an ideal and satisfying way to try out knotting patterns, and to test yarn qualities. And this in effect is their primary purpose, but it seems such a pity to banish all these attractive pieces of knotting to the work basket afterwards. In fact there are many ways samplers can be put to good use, both decorative and functional, so the world may see and admire them!

One of the simplest ideas is merely to mount your samplers on wooden rods and use as wall hangings. Or make pictures from them by mounting on a plain linen or other fabric background, and then framing them. The group of pictures shown opposite were originally samplers worked in synthetic twines, linen threads and raffia, which were subsequently framed.

Alternatively, a sampler can be combined with other materials and used as a central motif on a bag, dress or cushion cover. This can give a garment or household furnishing a new lease of life — a central worn area in a seat cover, for instance, can be covered with a decorative sampler. Or a torn or stained garment can be cleverly disguised.

The belt below and the string doll on page 162 show two original ways of putting samplers to good use. Both designs are based on sections of different knotting patterns but have of course been worked to a particular size and shape to suit the purpose of finished design.

If a sampler pattern consists of repeated motifs, more motifs can be added to extend the shape and size of sampler so it can be used for a particular purpose — either as a soft furnishing, or a fashion accessory.

Several small compatible samplers can be combined into a collage.

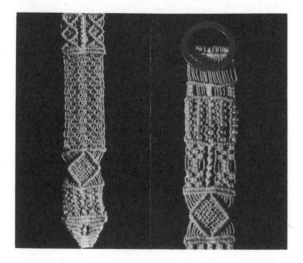

*Belt made from sampler in jute — patterned panels are separated by cording.*

*Opposte: nine samplers in polypropylene, raffia and string mounted on card to form attractive pictures.*

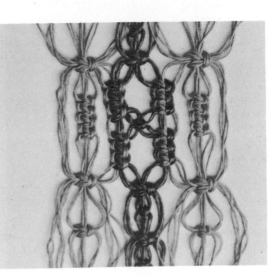

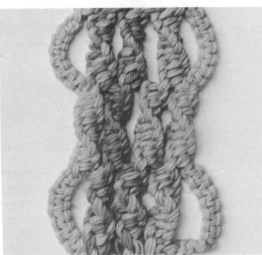

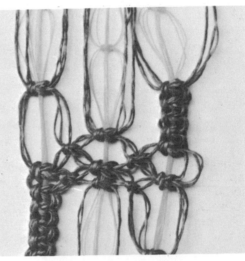

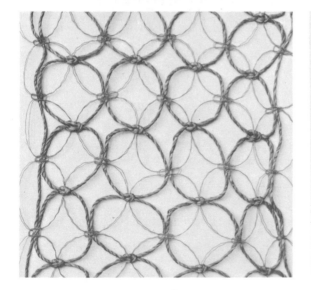

# Details that count

Macramé items need as much care and attention as any other form of textile, both in the making-up of composite designs and their after-care.

## PRESSING

Depending on the yarn used, and the knotting pattern, sometimes a light press on the wrong side of work is necessary especially for closely patterned pieces.

Pressing should be done in the way most suited to the yarn. Acrylic fibres normally do not require any pressing, but cotton, linen and wool usually do.

The method to use is this: place knotting right side down on a well-padded ironing board, and ease the knotting into its correct size and shape (a little gentle pulling may be needed to get all edges of a square item equal). Insert pins at right angles to work all round the edge. The closer the pins are the straighter the pressed edge will be. This process is similar to blocking.

When pinning is complete, press work using a warm iron over a damp cloth. Wait a few minutes until the steam has settled then remove the pins.

Synthetic fibres which do not require pressing can still be blocked by pinning out to shape, as described above. Then lay a damp cloth over the fabric, leaving until the cloth is completely dry.

## MAKING-UP

When making up garments by stitching (instead of combining with macramé knots) you can use either a flat or a backstitch seam. In either case, the yarn in which the knotting pattern was worked should be used (sometimes holding cords can be left deliberately

long and used for this purpose). If the yarn is too thick, then use sewing cotton.

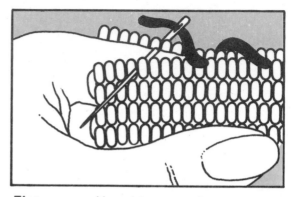

**Flat seam.** Use this seam for combining braids or putting on edgings. With right sides facing, place the two pieces of knotting together, edge to edge. Place the forefinger of your left hand just between these edges. Using an overcasting stitch draw the edges together over your finger. Move finger along as work proceeds.

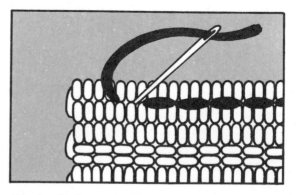

**Backstitch seam.** This seam should be used for edges where there will be extra pull or strain, such as side, shoulder and sleeve seams. With right sides of work together, backstitch seam as close to the edges as possible. Press all seams flat to finish.

## AFTER-CARE

Never allow any macramé item to get too dirty before washing. Careful washing – no matter how frequent – will never harm wool or man-made fibres. String items are the easiest to wash of all: a dunk in rich soapy lather followed by a good rinse will bring string items up fresh and sparkling. If the string has been dyed, be sure to wash it separately from other items.

### Washing woollen items

Wash woollen items gently in lukewarm soapy water; rinse thoroughly in at least three changes of warm water. Always support a woollen item with both hands while it is wet or it will stretch out of shape from its own weight. Gently squeeze the item after its final rinse, and roll it in a clean dry white towel without twisting. Leave to dry flat on a clean towel away from direct sunlight or strong artificial heat. Ease it into its correct shape and size. When dry, press lightly on the wrong side with a medium hot iron over a damp cloth. Heavy yarns such as rug wool need special care to prevent them from stretching.

### Washing cotton and linen

Wash in warm water and soap flakes; squeeze gently to remove dirt – never rub or twist. It may be necessary in the case of knotting worked to a specific shape such as a circle or a square to pin it out again (see pressing instructions opposite). If a light stiffening is required, use gum arabic or a solution of starch (1 dessertspoon to a pint of hot water); dab lightly over the article before pressing.

### Washing man-made fibres

Wash as for wool, press with a warm iron over a dry cloth. No pressing at all is required for Courtelle, Acrilan, Tricel or Orlon yarns. Plastic and similar twines need only an occasional sponge over with a soapy cloth.

## DYEING

Because so many of the best macramé knotting yarns come only in a natural shade, it is worth dyeing batches of your favourite yarns, and so giving a wider colour range than would otherwise be possible.

Most cotton and linen yarns dye well, so do all forms of twine and string. Many of the items shown throughout the book are made from ordinary parcel string which has been dyed – the chess set on page 72 has half its pieces made from black-dyed string, the other half from cream-dyed string. The belts on page 90 similarly are made from dyed parcel string in assorted colours.

When dyeing yarn, make sure you dye more than enough at a time for the project you intend working on. Over-estimate rather than under-estimate, even at the risk of being extravagant – for a second dyeing of a subsidiary quantity of yarn rarely produces exactly the same depth and quality of colour as the first dyeing.

This applies as much to coloured yarns bought from shops – it is always best to buy a sufficient quantity of the same dye lot all at once, as colours vary as much with professionally dyed yarns as with home dyeing.

There are many excellent proprietary brands of dyes on the market, including multi-purpose dyes which can be used for any type of yarn, and also cold water dyes and tints when strong colour is not required.

Choose a dye to suit your purpose and follow the instructions on the packet or tin implicitly.

Dyeing yarn in its loose state presents a different set of problems from dyeing made-up pieces of work. In order that yarn receives equal coverage, it should be loosely tied together in skeins with a piece of fine cotton, and the skein moved about in the dye solution with a wooden spoon so dye can soak into every surface area. Make sure the dye container is big enough. A small amount of vinegar added to a cold-water dye solution should prevent fading of the colour.

A variegated colour effect can sometimes be quite effective – to produce 'mottling', wind skein of yarn fairly tightly, in an 'S' bend.

Items can also be dyed in entirety after knotting is complete. If natural coloured wooden beads are part of the work, then they too will take on a tint of the dye colour. Individual parts of work can be painted with a fairly strong concentrate of dye solution after work is finished where areas of localised or stronger colour are required.

# The patterns

## Ring belt

Illustrated on page 144
**YARN.** Multicoloured synthetic cord.
**YOU WILL ALSO NEED.** 2 white plastic rings, each 2 in. in diameter.
**MEASUREMENT.** Finished belt should fit an average 24/26 in. waist. For each additional inch required, add a further 8 in. to cut thread lengths.
**PREPARATION.** Cut 6 threads, each $14\frac{1}{2}$ ft. Double them and set them with reversed double half hitches on to one plastic ring (have knot of reversed double half hitches on wrong side of work): 12 working ends.
**TO MAKE.** Work three 5-knot sinnets of flat knots with each group of 4 cords.
*Next row: leave first 2 cords unworked; work two 2-knot sinnets of flat knots; leave final 2 cords unworked.
**Next row:** work three 5-knot sinnets of flat knots.** Repeat from * to ** until belt is of desired length.
**TO FINISH.** Turn belt to wrong side, lay remaining plastic ring close to knotting, and finish as for flat method on page 84.

## Multicolour string belt

Illustrated on page 144
**YARN.** 2-colour parcel string, in four different colourways.
**YOU WILL ALSO NEED** A $2\frac{1}{2}$-in. circular buckle.
**MEASUREMENT.** As for ring belt.
**PREPARATION.** Cut string into 18 ft. lengths: 2 in the same colourway, 1 in each of other three colourways. Double the threads and set them with reversed double half hitches on to buckle, positioning one of the 2 threads of the same colour in the centre, the other at the far right.
**TO MAKE.** With cord on far left as leader, work 1 row of horizontal cording.
Work 5 rows of close diagonal cording slanting down to the right, using the outside left-hand cord as leader for each row.
*Now work 5 rows of close diagonal cording slanting down to the left, using the outside right-hand cord as leader for each row. Work 5 rows of close diagonal cording slanting down to the right, using the outside left-hand cord as leader for each row.**
Repeat from * to ** 3 times (or until work is long enough to fit your waist).
Now work 20 rows of close diagonal cording slanting down to the left, using outside right-hand cord as leader for each row.
**TO FINISH.** Turn work to wrong side, and work a final row of cording immediately below the last one, using cord on the far left as leader. Trim ends to about $\frac{1}{2}$ in. from knotting, and press them on to wrong side of belt. Add a spot of fabric glue, or a strip of self-adhesive tape to keep them in place.

# Three-colour belt

Illustrated on page 144
**YARN.** Double knitting wool in green, purple and orange (or any three colours).
**MEASUREMENT.** As for ring belt.
**PREPARATION.** Cut yarn into lengths of 15 ft.: 12 in green, 4 in orange, 4 in purple. Arrange cords on working surface in the following order: 6 green, 4 orange, 4 purple, 6 green. (**Note.** Do not double threads, but pin them singly to your working surface.) Tie an overhand knot with all cords about 36 in. from their ends. Pin to working surface through the overhand knot.

**TO MAKE.** Working from the overhand knot down, work in the alternate flat knot pattern throughout until belt is of the required length.
**TO FINISH.** Tie an overhand knot to combine all cords immediately below knotting. Working on the ends below the overhand knot, divide cords into 4 groups of cords: 2 groups of 6 green cords, 1 group of 4 orange, and 1 group of 4 purple.
Work flat knot sinnets with each group to measure approximately 8 in., or length required. Work the 6-cord sinnets (green) with 4 central knot-bearing core cords. Work similar flat knot sinnets with the cords at the beginning of belt.

# Josephine knot belt 1

Illustrated near right
**YARN.** Medium weight fishing line.
**YOU WILL ALSO NEED.** An interlocking belt clasp.
**MEASUREMENT.** To fit an average waist size of 24/26 in. For each additional inch of waist measurement, add 8 in. to lengths of cord cut.
**TENSION CHECK.** Each Josephine knot measures approximately $1\frac{3}{4}$ in. wide, 1 in. deep.
**PREPARATION.** Cut 2 cords, each 16 ft. Double them and set on with reversed double half hitches to one section of the belt clasp (4 working ends).
**TO MAKE.** Working with double strands of cord, work in Josephine knots throughout, tying each knot close to the last and reversing the direction of alternate knots — i.e. tie first knot by making the first loop in right-hand cords; begin second knot by making first loop in left-hand cords — and so on.
**TO FINISH.** Turn work to wrong side, place second half of belt clasp close to last knot and finish by flat knot method, page 84.

*Josephine belts 1 (see above) and 2 (see overleaf).*

# Josephine knot belt 2

Illustrated on page 141, right

**YARN.** Thick synthetic rope.

**MEASUREMENT.** To fit an average waist size of 24/26 in. For each additional inch of waist measurement, add 2 in. to each cord cut.

**TENSION CHECK.** Each Josephine knot measures 3½ in. wide, 3 in. deep.

**PREPARATION.** Cut 2 cords, each 20 ft. Double one and pin it by its looped end to your working surface. Double the second cord and place it on top of the first cord, so the top loop of second cord extends 3 in. beyond the first, and allow the working ends of first cord to lie on either side of the working ends of second cord. Tie a flat knot with the ends of first cord round ends of second cord. Pin to working surface through the flat knot.

**TO MAKE.** Leave 3 in. of cord unworked, then using double strands of cord, tie a Josephine knot. Leave another 3 in. of cords unworked and tie a second Josephine knot. Continue in this way until you have tied 4 Josephine knots.

Leave a further 3 in. of cord unworked and tie a collecting knot with one cord round the other three.

**Note.** For a bigger waist size, add extra measurement to area of unworked cords between second and third knots.

Similarly, if you wish to reduce measurement, subtract length from this area of cords.

**TO FINISH.** Unravel plies of cord ends to form fringed tassel at end. To fasten belt, the collecting knot is put through the loop at other end of belt.

# Hipster string belt

Illustrated right

**YARN.** Heavy parcel string.

**MEASUREMENT.** Finished belt is approximately 2 in. wide. It is designed to sit round the hips and because of the flexible nature of the front tie fastening, the belt should fit most figure sizes and shapes.

**TENSION CHECK.** Sinnet of 3 flat knots measures 1 inch long, ½ in. wide.

**PREPARATION.** Cut 2 threads, each 16 in. Double one of the threads then twist looped end round and down to form an oval coil approximately 1½ in. deep.

Pin this coil to your working surface so the loose ends hang down on either side of the coil. Double the other 16-in. thread and set it with a reversed double half hitch on to lower edge of coil between the 2 loose ends. Now tie a triple knot with the 4 ends, using the ends from the coil as knotting cords, the set-on ends as the central knot-bearing core. With the same 4 ends tie a flat knot about an inch down from the triple knot.

This oval loop thus formed will be the centre back of belt, and is used as a holding cord — working cords are set on down each side of

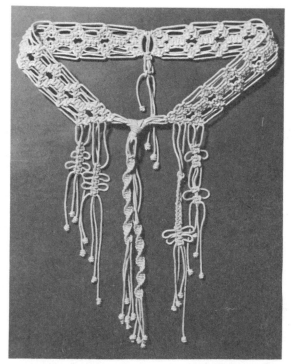

*Above: hipster string belt.*
*Opposite: rug wool shawl (see page 155).*

the oval, and worked out in each direction. Cut 12 threads, each 12 ft. long. Double them and set them with reversed double half hitches on to oval holding cord, 6 cords to each side. Unpin loop from working surface and re-pin so working cords for right-hand of belt hang down. You should have 12 working ends at each side.

**TO MAKE. 1st row:** work a flat knot with each 4 ends (3 knots altogether).

**2nd row:** leave first 2 cords unworked; work 2 flat knots; leave last 2 cords unworked.

**\*Next row:** leave first 4 cords unworked; work a 3-knot sinnet of flat knots with centre 4 cords; leave last 4 cords unworked.

**Next row:** as 2nd row.

**Next row:** work 1 flat knot; leave next 4 cords unworked; work 1 flat knot.

**Next row:** as 2nd row.\*\*

Repeat from \* to \*\* 7 more times.

**Next row:** leave first 4 cords unworked; work 2 flat knots.

**Next row:** work a flat knot between 2 knots of previous row.

**Next row:** work a flat knot with last 4 cords only.

Divide cords into groups of 4. Work any form of sinnet on the first and second groups of cords — our belt shows short sinnets of flat knots with picots. Unpin work, and re-pin to working surface so working ends for left-hand side of belt hang down.

Work exactly as for right-hand side as far as \*\*.

**Next row:** work 2 flat knots; leave last 4 cords unworked.

**Next row:** work 1 flat knot between 2 knots of previous row.

**Next row:** work 1 flat knot with first 4 cords.

Divide cords into groups of 4, and work any form of sinnet on the second and third groups of cords.

Unpin work and link the unworked groups of 4 cords from each side together by tying with a sliding knot (as used to knot a necktie).

Allow the knot to slide to extent required to put belt on, and then finish the ends below sliding knot with 2 banister bars.

**TO FINISH.** Work a coil knot at the bottom of every loose cord, including the 4 at centre back.

# *Beaded choker*

Illustrated on right

**YARN.** Synthetic tubular cord.

**YOU WILL ALSO NEED.** 14 wooden beads in a colour to match or contrast with yarn.

**MEASUREMENT.** Finished choker measures approximately 1 in. wide, 13 in. long (or length required to fit neck), excluding beaded fringe.

**PREPARATION.** Cut 7 threads, 3 at 2 ft. 6 in., 4 at 6 ft. Arrange threads on working surface so the 3 short ends are in the centre, with 2 long ends on either side. Tie all cords together with an overhand knot, positioning knot about 5 in. from the ends of cords. Pin to working surface through overhand knot.

*Opposite, top picture, top to bottom: multi-colour string belt, ring belt, three-colour belt (see pages 140–41); left: multi-coloured table mat (see page 158); bottom right: square patterns 1 (left), 2 (centre) and 3.*

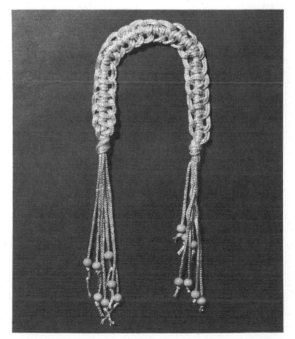

**TO MAKE.** Work a Genoese bar (half hitches worked alternately from each side over a central core), working knots with double strands over the central three-cord core. Continue until the choker is long enough to fit comfortably round neck (approximately 12 in.).

Tie all the cords together with an overhand knot.

**TO FINISH.** Trim ends to same length as fringe at the beginning. Thread a bead on to each end and tie overhand knots in each cord to hold bead in place. If wished, use more than one bead on each cord.

# *Lacy hairband*

Illustrated on right

**YARN.** Fine white nylon cord (normally sold in hardware stores and departments for light or bell pulls).

**YOU WILL ALSO NEED.** Approximately 12 in. of narrow elastic.

**MEASUREMENT.** Finished knotted braid is 11 in. long, 1 in. wide.

**TENSION CHECK.** One motif measures approximately 1 inch square.

**PREPARATION.** Cut 3 threads, each 8 ft., cut 4 threads, each 4 ft. Double the 8 ft. cords and set them with reversed double half hitches on to a holding cord about 6 in. long (6 working ends).

**TO MAKE.** Using cord on the far left as leader, work 1 row of horizontal cording. Reverse direction of leader round a pin and work a second row of horizontal cording. Pin one of 4 ft. lengths of cord close to left-hand side of work, and using this cord as a leader work horizontal cording across all cords.

Now pin another 4 ft. length close to right-hand side of work, and using this as a leader, work horizontal cording right across. The leader from the previous row becomes the first knotting cord in this row. In a similar way, introduce the third 4 ft. length of cord in the next row, and the last 4 ft. length in the row after that.

**Pattern motif:** the 5th cord from the left-hand side is used as a leader to form diagonal cording slanting down to the left.

Pin it in position across work, and knot cords 4, 3, 2 and 1 over it.

In a similar way work diagonal cording slanting down to the right using cord 6 as leader, and knotting cords 7, 8, 9 and 10 over it.

Now tie a flat knot in the centre with cords

3, 4, 7 and 8.

**Next row:** tie a flat knot with cords 1, 2, 3 and 4, and another flat knot with cords 7, 8, 9 and 10.

**Next row:** tie a flat knot with cords 3, 4, 7 and 8.

Continuing to use cord 5 as a leader, reverse its direction round a pin and work diagonal cording slanting to the right, with cords 1, 2, 3 and 4.

Similarly work diagonal cording slanting to the left with cords 10, 9, 8 and 7 over cord 6. Reverse directions of leaders round pins and repeat motif, allowing unworked areas of cords at the sides (between the motifs) to form gentle and regular curves.

Continue in this way until 9 motifs in all have been worked.

Using cord on the far left as leader, work a second row of horizontal cording immediately below the first. At the end of this row pin leader out of the way, and work a third row of cording, using cord on far left as leader. Again at the end of this row, pin leader out of the way and work a fourth row of cording with cord on far right as leader. (Width of work should be gradually decreasing with each successive row.)

This leader too is no longer required, and the final 2 rows of cording are worked using the cord on the far left as leader for the first row, then reversing its direction round a pin so it continues as leader for the second row.

**TO FINISH.** Withdraw holding cord from set-on edge. Trim all ends to about $\frac{3}{4}$ in. (including leader cords) and weave into back of work, or take the cords at each end of braid to the back of work, lay them flat together against back of knotting, and with a needle and fine cotton thread, secure to back of knotting with a few neat stitches.

Stitch one narrow end of elastic to each end of knotted braid.

# Two-colour tote bag

Illustrated on right

**YARN.** Medium-weight parcel string in a dark and a light shade.

**YOU WILL ALSO NEED.** 2 wooden rings, each 6 in. in diameter.

**MEASUREMENT.** Finished bag measures approximately 24 in. long (including handles), and 17 in. across at widest point.

**TENSION CHECK.** Width of 1 flat knot is $\frac{3}{8}$ in.

**PREPARATION.** Using light-coloured string, work half hitches over each ring, knotting over cord ends so the wooden ring is completely and closely covered by strands of string. Have the knot of the half hitches round outer edge of rings.

Cut 32 threads in light colour, 16 in dark, each 12 ft. long. Double them and set 16 light and 8 dark on to one of the prepared rings with reversed double half hitches in the following colour sequence: 5 light, 4 dark, 6 light, 4 dark, 5 light.

Set remaining threads in a similar way on to the other prepared ring.

**TO MAKE.** Work on one ring only:

\***1st row**: work in flat knots across row (12 knots altogether).

**2nd row**: leave first 2 cords unworked, work 11 flat knots, and leave final 2 cords unworked.

Continue to work in the alternate flat knot pattern until you have worked 7 rows altogether. The first rows should be worked fairly tightly and close together but as you work down, gradually increase distance be-

*Tote bag is worked in two colours of string.*

tween knots and rows, to give more width at sides of work. **

Work from * to ** on second ring.

Now link the two pieces of knotting together: place both sections of knotting together, so side edges align, and wrong sides are facing (have knots of reversed double half hitches along set-on edges on the inside).

Work now continues in the round, so you will no longer be able to work on a flat surface, but will need a padded block of wood or other suitable shape as a support.

Continuing the alternate sequence, work flat knots right round work, so each pair of cords at the edges of side 1 are knotted with the corresponding pair of cords from side 2: there will be 24 knots in all in the row.

Continue working in the round in the alternate flat knot pattern until work is 18 in., or length required. Gradually increase distance between knots and rows to give more width to lower part of bag (if wished).

**TO FINISH.** Cut a length of light-coloured string, approximately 12 ft. long. Position finished knotting on its side so the bottom edge (which is to be closed) is running vertically. Beginning at the top of opening, loop the cut end of string round all the 8 ends coming from the last 2 flat knots.

Work a sinnet of flat knots, using this cut end of string as knotting cords, and loose ends from the completed knotting pattern as central knot-bearing core.

Continue to work a flat knot sinnet, catching in the loose ends from all the final row of knots as you come to them, so you gradually form a fairly bulky but solid closed edge along bottom of bag.

When you reach the end of the opening, continue to work the sinnet beyond the end of the bag for about an inch, then trim ends to about 2 in., to form a tassel.

# String envelope bag

Illustrated opposite, top

**YARN.** Parcel string, dyed if wished.

**YOU WILL ALSO NEED.** Piece of lining fabric, to match or contrast with knotting yarn, approximately 2 ft. long, 18 in. wide. One large bead or button.

**MEASUREMENT.** Finished bag measures approximately 9 in. wide, 7½ in. long, 1 in. deep.

Depth of flap: 5 in.

**PREPARATION.** Cut 44 threads each 12 ft., double them and set them with reversed double half hitches on to holding cord about 18 in. long (88 working ends).

**TO MAKE. Main section.** * **1st row:** work 4-end flat knots across all cords.

**2nd row:** leave first 2 cords unworked; tie flat knots across row to last 2 cords; leave these unworked. **

Repeat from * to ** twice more.

*** Now work on first 12 cords only:

Repeat from * to ** twice, then work a first pattern row.

Work on last 12 cords only:

Repeat from * to ** twice, then work a first pattern row.

Now work on centre 64 cords:

Work 6-knot sinnets of flat knots on each 4 cords (16 sinnets altogether). Now cross each pair of sinnets, crossing the first over the second, the fourth over the third, the fifth over the sixth, the eighth over the seventh, and so on. ****

Work a 2nd pattern row, across all cords, thus linking the side edges with the centre pattern section.

Repeat from *** to ****, but when you cross the sinnets over each other, reverse the crossing order (i.e. sinnet 2 over sinnet 1, sinnet 3 over sinnet 4, sinnet 6 over sinnet 5, sinnet 7 over sinnet 8 – and so on).

Work a first pattern row across all cords and continue in the alternate flat knot pattern until work measures 22 in.

Cut cords to within ½ in. of knotting.

**Handle.** Cut 6 threads each 30 ft. long. Double them and set them with reversed double half hitches on to a short holding cord (12 working ends). Work in the alternate flat knot pattern until work measures 42 in. Trim ends to within ½ in. of knotting.

*Opposite, top: string envelope bag; bottom: beaded bag (see page 150).*

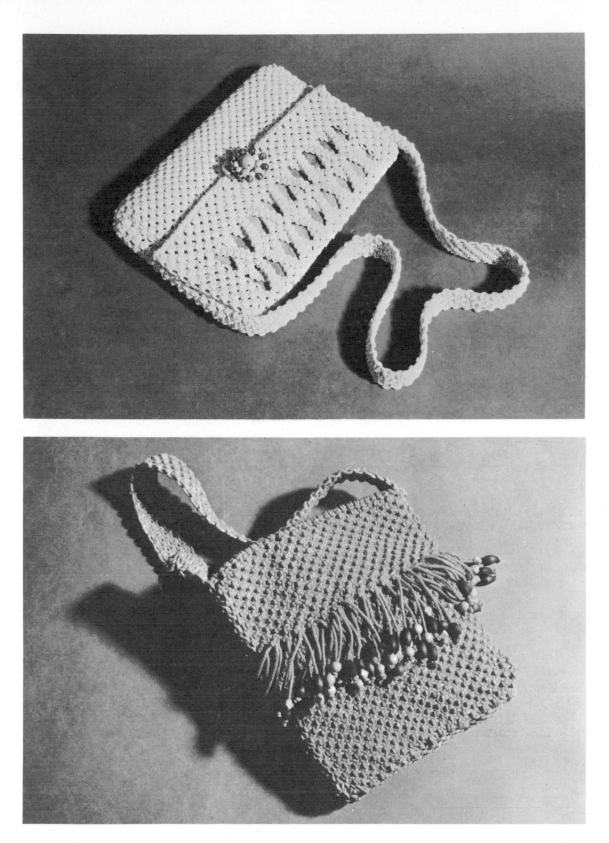

**TO FINISH.** Fold main knotted section in three, so section with crossed-sinnet pattern forms a flap of approximately 5 in., the other two folds are about 7½ in. each, and a 1 in. depth is allowed between the folds (for depth of bag). Now position the handle against the folded section to form side gussets of bag, and stitch in place round sides and lower edge. Trim holding cord to within an inch of either side of work and turn ends to wrong side.

Make up lining to fit bag, including the flap section. Place it wrong sides facing inside bag, and stitch neatly in place, being sure to enclose loose ends of knotting, and of holding cord.

Stitch decorative bead or button to centre front of main section just below flap. Work a sinnet of flat knots to fit comfortably round bead or button and stitch this to centre of flap opposite button.

# Beaded bag

Illustrated on page 149, bottom picture
**YARN.** Parcel string, dyed if wished.
**YOU WILL ALSO NEED.** 68 wooden beads.
**MEASUREMENT.** Finished bag measures approximately 9 in. square, with a 1½ in. side and bottom gusset. Handle is 28 in. long.
**PREPARATION.** Main section: cut 34 threads, each 80 in. Double them and set them with reversed double half hitches on to a holding cord approximately 15 in. long (68 working ends). Handle: cut 6 threads, each 40 ft. long. Double them and set them with reversed double half hitches on to a short holding cord (12 working ends).
**TO MAKE. Main section (make 2 pieces alike).** Work in the alternate flat knot pattern for 41 rows or to length required.
Cut ends to within 1 in. of knotting.
Now cut 17 threads, each 12 in. Count down 14 rows from start of work and on the 15th row, loop a 12-in. strand round each flat knot. Tie two 2-end flat knots (i.e. no central core)

with each strand on the right side of work. Thread a bead on to the end of each strand and tie an overhand knot to hold bead in position.
**Handle.** Work in alternate flat knots pattern for 55 in., or to length required (the handle must be long enough to go right round sides and bottom of bag as well as provide a carrying handle).
**TO FINISH.** Sew short ends of handle strip together to form a circle, or pull each cord end through the set-on edge, and tie in pairs of 2-end flat knots on the wrong side. Now position the 2 main sections, one on either side of handle, so the handle strip forms side and bottom gussets of bag, and with beading on outside of main sections. Stitch firmly together. Position handle 'seam' at one top corner of bag. Stitch firmly together, pushing holding cords to inside of bag as you come to them. Trim these holding cord ends to about 1 in., and glue them lightly to inside of bag.

# Victorian reticule bag

Illustrated opposite
**YARN.** Medium-weight waxed linen twine which is strong but slippery — any good quality medium twine would do instead.
**YOU WILL ALSO NEED.** A piece of lining fabric, about 14 in. square.
**MEASUREMENT.** Finished bag measures approximately 6 in. long, 5½ in. at widest point (excluding fringe).
**PREPARATION.** Cut a double thickness of

holding cord and tie ends together to form a circle approximately 8 in. in circumference (4 in. long if circle is doubled and laid flat). Cut 120 cords, each 6 ft. long. Double them and set them on in pairs with reversed double half hitches to the circular holding cord, and covering joined ends of holding cord. You now have 240 ends, but as the design is worked throughout in double strands, this constitutes only 120 working ends.

**Note.** This design is worked in the round, and – unless otherwise stated – with double strands of yarn.

**TO Make. 1st round:** flat knots right round, tying each knot with 4 double cords.

Divide cords into groups of 12 double strands for each motif. From now on, each double strand will be referred to as one working end, and each group of cords is numbered 1–12 for ease of identification.

Cord 1 of each group should be cord 3 of any flat knot in the row just worked.

**To work one complete motif:** work a flat knot with cords 5, 6, 7 and 8.

With cord 1 as leader, work the top curve of a leaf pattern slanting to the right with cords 2, 3, 4, 5 and 6.

Divide double strands of cord 3, and work a double half hitch with one strand over the other to form a horizontal bar across leaf.

Similarly divide double strands of cord 4, and work 2 double half hitches; then divide double strands of cord 5 and work 3 double half hitches.

Finally divide double strands of cord 6 and work 2 double half hitches.

Now using cord 2 (double thickness) as leader, form lower curve of leaf, slanting to the right, with cords 3, 4, 5 and 6.

Divide cords 2 and 1 into single strands, and tie a flat knot to close leaf with the 4 ends. You should now have a leaf motif, enclosing 4 horizontal bars.

In a similar way work a leaf motif with horizontal bars with cords 12, 11, 10, 9, 8 and 7, but slant motif to the left.

Link the 2 leaf motifs by tying a flat knot bead with cords 1, 2, 11 and 12 (tie 4 flat knots before taking sinnet up and over itself).

Work this motif across each group of 12 cords. Between each pair of motifs work 4 flat knots in alternate pattern (1 knot in first row, 2 in second, 1 in third).

Divide cords again into groups of 12: cord 1 of each group should be cord 11 from one of the previous round motifs.

Work motifs across each group of 12 in the same way.

Continue in this way until 4 rounds of motifs have been worked altogether.

**Next round:** work sinnets of 3 flat knots with cords coming from point where 2 leaves join, and also with cords between leaves – this means you will be working sinnets alter-

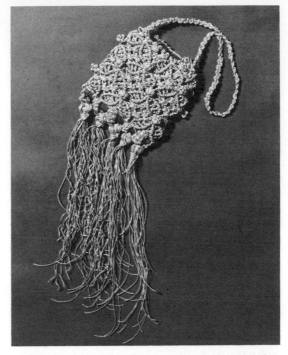

nately with 4 double strands, and 8 double strands. In the 8-end sinnets, use 2 outer pairs of cords for knotting, with 4 central knot-bearing core cords.

Take knotting off working base. Lay it on a flat surface and tie 5 multi-end flat knots across bottom of work, between sinnets and combining cords from the front with cords from the back.

**TO FINISH.** In each group of cords along lower edge, use one to tie a three-stranded collecting knot round the rest to form a tassel. Trim ends evenly, or leave them uneven if preferred.

Cut 2 threads, each 14 ft. Place threads together, double them and set on with a reversed double half hitch to top holding cord of bag at point where you wish one end of handle to be positioned.

Work a double alternate half hitch chain almost to the end of cords, then attach to holding cord of bag at opposite side with a double half hitch.

Tuck loose ends of handle inside bag.

Make up lining for bag with lining material, and place inside bag, wrong sides together, and sandwiching loose ends of knotted handle.

Hemstitch neatly round top edge.

# Square motifs

Attractive square motifs can be made from many different knotting patterns. According to the yarn type and weight used, these may be made up into a variety of useful and decorative items. Several together can be linked either with knotted braids, embroidery stitches or neat hand or machine stitching and formed into any of the following items: patchwork bolero, coat or dress; fashion trimming (from a strip of squares); bag; baby's shawl (from squares made in a fine wool in white or pastel shade); cushion cover; bedspread. The patterns which follow give three different versions of square patterns. Each is worked in double knitting wool to give a square of approximately 4 in. If you are making squares for a bedspread or similar large item, you may prefer to work in a thicker yarn — rug wool, for instance, or a thicker ply — in order to achieve bigger squares. On the other hand if smaller finer squares are wanted, for a dressing table mat perhaps, or lacy trimming, then use a fine crochet cotton, a rayon, or even silk embroidery thread.

## Square 1

Illustrated page 144 (bottom left square).
**YARN.** Double knitting wool.
**MEASUREMENT.** Finished square measures approximately 4 in.
**PREPARATION.** Cut 14 threads, each 32 in. long. Double them and mount them with reversed double half hitches to a holding cord approximately 10 in. long (you now have 28 working ends).
**TO MAKE.** Using cord on the far left as leader, work a double row of horizontal cording.

* **Next row:** sinnets of 2 flat knots across row.
**Next row:** work 2 reversed double half hitches with cord 1 over cord 2.
Work 6 sinnets of 2-knot flat knots.
Work 2 reversed double half hitches with the last cord over the second-last cord. * *
Repeat from * to * * twice more.
Using cord on the far right as leader, work a double row of horizontal cording.
**TO FINISH.** Trim ends ¾ in. from knotting, press to back of work and weave through last row of knots.

## Square 2

Illustrated page 144 (top square).
**YARN.** Double knitting wool.
**MEASUREMENT.** Finished square measures approximately 4 in.
**PREPARATION.** Cut 6 threads in colour A, each 24 in. long. Double them and set them on to a circular holding cord by Method 1 on page 97. Tighten circle until holding cord is completely concealed.
**TO MAKE. 1st round:** work flat knots with each 4 ends.
Introduce a new circular holding cord in colour B, laying it under working cords.
Cut 6 threads in colour B, each 18 in.

Double them and set them with reversed double half hitches on to new holding cord, positioning 2 new cords (4 ends) between colour A sinnets.
**Next round:** work 4-end flat knots right round (6 knots), combining 2 cords of colour A with 2 cords of colour B for each knot.
**Next round:** work 4-end flat knots in alternate sequence from last round (i.e. each knot will use cords in the same colour — 1 knot in colour A, 1 knot in colour B, and so on).
Introduce another circular holding cord, this time in colour C. Cut 12 cords in colour C, each 15 in., and set them on with reversed

double half hitches, 2 between each knot of previous round.

**Next round:** flat knots right round (12 knots): knot in colour A, knot in colour C, knot in colour B, knot in colour C — and so on.

**Next round:** flat knots in alternate sequence so 2 cords of one colour are knotted with 2 cords of the colour next to it.

Repeat last 2 rounds once.

Work 1 flat knot at each corner of square — there will be 1 knot in colour A and 1 knot in colour B, at opposite corners, and a knot in colour C at each of the other two corners.

Attach a separate leader approximately 8 in. long and work a row of horizontal cording at each side of the square to 'contain' it (attach a separate leader for each row, and knot leader of previous row on to the new leader each time).

**TO FINISH.** Trim ends to $\frac{3}{4}$ in. from knotting. Weave in ends to back of work, including ends from leaders used for edging.

**Note.** This square will have to be pinned carefully as you work in order to keep it flat — it has a natural tendency to curve round on itself.

# Square 3

Illustrated page 144 (bottom right square).
**YARN.** Double knitting wool.
**MEASUREMENT.** Finished square measures approximately 4 in.
**PREPARATION.** As for Square 1.
**TO MAKE.** * **1st row:** 2-knot sinnets of flat knots across row.
**2nd row:** leave first 2 cords unworked; work 6 banister bars, knotting 6 half knots in each

bar; leave final 2 cords unworked. * *
Repeat from * to * * three times. * * *
**Last row:** as first row.
**TO FINISH.** As for Square 1.
**Note.** If a number of squares are to be combined, ends should not be trimmed, but can be used to knot to ends of adjoining square, if wished.

# Square motif bag

Illustrated on page 154
**YARN.** Double knitting wool.
**YOU WILL ALSO NEED.** 1 yard of lining fabric, 18 in. wide.
**MEASUREMENT.** Finished bag measures approximately 12 in. by 16 in., plus 4 in. fringe.
Handle: $1\frac{1}{2}$ in. wide, 2 ft. long.
**TO MAKE. Main section.** Make 18 squares in Square 3 pattern (see above).
Make 6 more squares, but cut threads 36 in. long, and follow instructions for Square 3 only as far as * * *.
Take 2 of these squares, place them together, wrong sides facing, and work 2-knot sinnets of 8-end flat knots across, so 4 cords from each square are combined in each knot: 2 outer pairs of knotting cords, 4 central knot-bearing core cords.
Repeat with other 2 pairs of squares.

**Handle.** Cut 8 threads, each 16 ft. long and set them with reversed double half hitches on to a holding cord approximately 8 in. long (16 working ends).
Work double alternate half hitch chains to a depth of 1 in. on each group of 4 cords.
Now work in alternate flat knot pattern, 2 knots to each row, until handle measures 23 in. (or length required).
Work double alternate half hitch chains to a depth of 1 in. on each group of 4 cords.
**TO FINISH.** Each side of the bag consists of 4 rows of 3 squares. Stitch each strip of 3 squares together first: lay the squares right side up on your working surface so edges are even, then thread a darning needle with the yarn used for knotting, and overcast edges of squares together, stitching over the unworked loops along each side edge.
The linked squares which will form the lower

edge of bag are stitched together in a similar way.

Now stitch the strips of squares together to form each side of the bag. Position the linked squares at lower edge. Again, work on the right side, and use overcasting stitches to combine the lower edge of one strip with the top (set-on) edge of the next. Loose ends of knotting should be pushed to wrong side of work before stitching begins. After stitching is complete, turn work to wrong side and knot each pair of ends into 2-end flat knots, and trim ends neatly.

Finally stitch side edges of bag together. Stitch handle in place.

Cut 2 pieces of lining, each 13 in. by 17 in. Place together, right sides facing, and stitch round both long sides and one short side, taking $\frac{1}{2}$ in. turnings. Trim and clip turnings and turn lining right side out. Place in bag, wrong sides together, turn in $\frac{1}{2}$ in. along top edge of lining, and hemstitch neatly to inside of bag. A strip of lining may be stitched along inside of handle if wished.

Trim fringe evenly to 4 in. or to depth of fringe required.

# Rug wool shawl

Illustrated on page 143
**YARN.** Rug wool.

**MEASUREMENT.** Finished shawl measures approximately 56 in. at longest edge of triangle, approximately 30 in. deep to point (excluding fringe).

**TENSION CHECK.** One 4-end flat knot measures about $\frac{3}{4}$ in. across.

**PREPARATION.** Cut a holding cord approximately 135 in. long. Tie an overhand knot 52 in. from each end and pin to working surface.

Now cut 36 threads to the lengths which follow, double them and set them on to holding cord by simple picot edging in this order (left to right): 3 ft., 3 ft. 4 in., 3 ft. 8 in., 4 ft., and so on, increasing by 4 in. each time, to 8 ft. 8 in., then the next thread is 9 ft., then 9 ft. 3 in., 9 ft. 6 in., and so on, increasing by 3 in each time to final cord of 13 ft. 3 in.

You now have 72 working ends.

Prepare a second (separate) holding cord in a similar way, but work this time from right to left, so the 3 ft. cord will be at far right, the 13 ft. 3 in. cord on the far left.

**TO MAKE. Work on first triangle.** Work 4-end flat knots across row.

**2nd row:** leave first 2 cords unworked then work flat knots across row to last 2 cords; leave them unworked.

**3rd row:** leave first 2 cords unworked, then work flat knots across row to last 2 cords; leave them unworked.

*Opposite: square motif bag (see page 153).*

Continue in this way, dropping 2 cords from each side on each successive row until eventually you will work a row with one knot only in it.

Unpin holding cord from left-hand side, untie overhand knot. Place a pin in working surface close to top left-hand side of work, and take holding cord round it.

Work cording down left-hand side of triangle, close to knotting and using holding cord as leader.

Now work second triangle in a similar way, but work row of cording down right-hand side, and use holding cord from the right as leader.

Place both triangles together so top edge forms a continuous line and cording edges are on the outside. Untie overhand knots in both holding cords, loop the 2 cords round each other so corners of triangle are linked closely at the top edge, then work cording down right-hand side of triangle 1 with its holding cord as leader, and cording down left-hand side of triangle 2 with its holding cord as leader.

You now have 72 working ends between the two worked triangles.

Knot pattern as follows:

**1st row:** one 4-end flat knot.

**Next row:** 2 flat knots (bringing in 2 ends from cording at either side).

**Next row:** 3 flat knots (bringing in 2 more ends from cording at either side).

Continue in this way to work an inverted triangle until you work the row with 18 flat knots in it.

**Next row:** leave first 2 cords unworked; work flat knots across row to last 2 cords; leave them unworked.

Continue to decrease in this way, as for triangles 1 and 2, until you finally work the row with only 1 flat knot in it.

Work cording down left-hand edge of triangle continuing from the point of triangle 1 and using the same leader cord as before. The leader which was used to work cording down right-hand edge of triangle 1 will become a knotting cord and will be knotted over the leader. Work cording down remaining right-hand edge of shawl in a similar way.

At the tip of the triangle knot one leader over the other (it does not matter which).

**TO FINISH.** Trim fringe evenly to 10 in., or depth required.

# *Matching headscarf*

Illustrated below
**YARN.** Rug wool.
**MEASUREMENT.** Finished headscarf measures approximately 28 in. at longest edge; 15 in. to tip of triangle (excluding fringe).
**TENSION CHECK.** As for rug wool shawl.
**PREPARATION.** Cut holding cord about 100 in. Tie an overhand knot about 35 in. from each end and pin to working surface. Cut 36 cords to the lengths which follow, double

them and set them on to holding cord by simple picot edging in this order (from left to right): 3 ft., 3 ft. 4 in., 3 ft. 8 in., and so on, increasing by 4 in. each time to 8 ft. 8 in., set on another 8 ft. 8 in. thread, then decrease by 4 in. each time until final cord of 3 ft. You now have 72 working ends.
**TO MAKE.** Work in flat knots, as for shawl pattern, dropping 2 cords from each side on every row, until finally you work a row with

one flat knot only.

Unpin holding cord from left-hand side, untie overhand knot. Place pin in working surface beside top left-hand edge of knotting. Take holding cord round the pin and using it as leader, work cording down left-hand side of triangle.

In a similar way, work cording down right-hand edge of triangle with right-hand holding cord. At tip of triangle work cording with one leader over the other (it does not matter which).

**TO FINISH.** Trim fringe to 10 in., or depth required.

# *Sampler scarf*

Illustrated on right

**YARN.** Medium-weight cotton knitting yarn (dishcloth cotton is best).

**MEASUREMENT.** Finished scarf measures approximately 8 in. wide; length — as wished.

**TENSION CHECK.** Sinnet of 4 flat knots measures 1 in. long, $\frac{3}{8}$ in. wide.

**PREPARATION.** Cut 28 threads, each 8 times the finished length of scarf required, plus depth of fringing at one end — e.g. if you wish a finished scarf of 3 ft., with a 10-in. fringe at each end, cut threads each 24 ft. 10 in. (8 times 3, plus 10 in.). Double threads and set them on to a holding cord about 15 in. long with simple picot edging (small picots). You now have 56 working ends.

**TO MAKE.** Using cord on far left as leader, work a row of horizontal cording immediately below set-on edge. This gives the appearance (with double half hitches worked when setting on threads) of a double row of cording.

* **Pattern section 1. 1st row:** work 4-knot sinnets of flat knots across row (14 sinnets altogether).

**Divider rows:** using cord on far left as leader, work horizontal cording across row, reverse direction of leader round a pin, and work a second row of horizontal cording immediately below the previous one.

**Pattern section 2.** Work 8-end banister bars, tying 12 half knots in each bar, and letting the chain twist after every 4th knot: use 2 outer pairs of cords as knotting cords, 4 centre ones as the knot-bearing core (7 banister bars altogether).

**Divider rows:** as for the divider rows, pattern section 1.

**Pattern section 3.** Work 3 rows of alternate flat knot pattern.

**Divider rows:** as for divider rows, pattern section 1. **

Repeat from * to ** once.

Continue working in alternate bands of pattern sections 1 and 3, each time separating them with a double row of horizontal cording.

Continue until work is the length of scarf required minus 10 in. (e.g. if you wish a 36-in. scarf, excluding fringes, continue knotting until work measures 26 in.). End

with a pattern section 3. Work divider rows of horizontal cording then continue as follows:
Work pattern section 2, and divider rows.
Work pattern section 1, and divider rows.
Work pattern section 3, and divider rows.
Work pattern section 2, and divider rows.
Work pattern section 1, and divider rows.
**TO FINISH.** Trim fringe to depth required.

To make fringe at set-on edge, cut 28 threads each double the measurement of fringe required plus 1 in. (e.g. if a 10-in. fringe is required, cut the threads each 21 in.). Double the threads and set them on with reversed double half hitches to picot loops along set-on edge. Trim fringe evenly to match fringe at other end.

# Matching hat

(Not illustrated)
A matching hat may be made by working in the round over a suitable base — a wig stand, for instance, is ideal. Set on threads to a circular holding cord by Method 1 on page 97, and work in alternate bands of pattern sections 1 and 3, dividing each by a double row of horizontal cording, and adding new cords by double half hitches where needed in the cording rounds. A tasselled pompon may be sewn to the centre point afterwards if wished.

# Multicoloured table mat

Illustrated on page 144
**YARN.** Medium-weight cotton (dishcloth, preferably) in white and three toning or contrasting colours. Our mat is made in white, pink, pale blue and dark green.
**MEASUREMENT.** Finished mat measures approximately $5\frac{1}{2}$ in by 7 in., excluding fringe.
**TENSION CHECK.** 7 double half hitches on holding cord measure 1 in.
**PREPARATION.** Cut threads each 6 ft., in the following colours: 8 in white, 4 in blue, 4 in green, 4 in pink (or chosen colours). Double them and set them with simple picot edging on to a holding cord (any colour) about 12 in. long. Arrange the cords in the following order: 2 white, 1 green and 1 pink with their strands alternated so picot loops overlap (1 strand green, 1 pink, 1 green, 1 pink), 2 blue, 1 pink and 1 green with strands alternated and picots overlapping, 4 white, 1 green and 1 pink with strands alternated and picots overlapping, 2 blue, 1 pink and 1 green with strands alternated and picot loops overlapping, 2 white.
**TO MAKE.** Pin separate leader (any colour) approximately 12 in. long to left-hand side and work horizontal cording over it across

row (you now have 2 rows of horizontal cording).
Begin diagonal cording pattern:
Cord 2 (white) as leader slanting to left, diagonal cording over it with cord 1 (white).
Cord 4 (white) as leader slanting to the left, diagonal cording over it with cords 3, 1 and 2 (all white).
* Cord 6 (pink) as leader slanting to the left, diagonal cording with cord 5 (green). Continue in this way using every even-numbered cord as leader, slanting to the left, and working diagonal cording over it with every cord as far as edge of green section (cord 5 will be outer knotting cord).
When the last white cord of centre section has been used as a leader, begin this knotting sequence from * again with next group of cords, First knotting cord will again be green, and stop when each of the 4 white cords have been used as leader. Go back to left-hand side of work and work a pink, blue and green section in cording slanting to the right.
First leader will then be the 4th white cord from the left, and 2 pink, 2 blue and 2 green cords are knotted over it.
Next row will have the 3rd white cord as

leader, and again 2 pink, 2 blue and 2 green are knotted over it.

A similar pattern is worked over the 2nd white cord, and then the first white cord. Then each of the cords at the far left in pink, blue and green are used until the row is worked where one green cord only is knotted over the other green cord.

Continue with 4 rows of cording below this section, using as leaders each of cords slanting down to the left from the section of cording already worked, and working from right to left. As each row is worked the leader from this row will become a knotting cord in the subsequent row.

Work 4 rows in all, taking cording across to the left-hand edge. Now work next section starting at point just below set-on edge and working from right to left: use each cord slanting from left to right as leaders, knotting over them with pink, blue and green cords.

Work 14 rows altogether (until last white cord of 2nd group of white cords has been used as a leader). Continue working in this direction, but use cords slanting down to left as leaders and work 6 rows of cording (pink, blue and green).

Complete this section as far as left-hand side of work by using cords slanting to the right as leaders, and knotting pink, blue and green cords over them in turn right to the edge of work.

The next 4 rows slanting all the way across work are knotted from right to left over cords slanting down to the left. On the 4th row stop knotting one cord from the end.

Below this section, from right to left pattern sequence is as follows: leaders used slanting down to the right, stripes worked in pink, blue and green until the 4th white cord has been used as leader. Then leaders are taken slanting down to the left, and 6 rows worked (pink, blue and green); the leaders taken slanting down to the right, and 14 rows worked (pink, blue and green). Leaders taken slanting to the left and rows worked thus:

**Next row:** 2 pink double half hitches, 2 blue, 2 green.
**Next row:** 2 pink, 2 blue, 1 green.
**Next row:** 2 pink, 2 blue.
**Next row:** 2 pink, 1 blue.
**Next row:** 2 pink.
**Next row:** 1 pink.

Next 4 rows are knotted over cords slanting down to the left across work. At lower edge drop one knot each time.

**Next section:** use cords slanting to the right as leaders as far as the 4th white cord (working from right to left) and work pink, blue and green cords in turn.

Complete section below this by knotting over cords slanting to the left, dropping one knot each time at lower edge.

Complete lower right-hand corner by knotting 3 rows of white over cords slanting to the left — 3 knots in first row, 2 in second, 1 in third.

Pin separate leader to left-hand side of work (any colour), approximately 2 ft. long and work a double row of horizontal cording.

**TO FINISH.** Trim lower cords to form fringe approximately 2 in. or depth required.

Cut threads, each 6 in. in following colours: 8 white, 4 each of other three colours. Double cords and set each on by reversed double half hitch to picot loops along set-on edge, matching strand colour to picot colour. Trim this fringe to match lower edge fringe. Trim ends of leader cords and holding cords, and turn them to wrong side of work. Secure along back of cording rows with a few neat stitches.

# Victorian panel

Illustrated on page 160

In Victorian days, panels such as this were knotted to hang in front of shelves, corner cupboards, brackets or small mantelpieces. Today the design can serve a similar purpose, or may merely be used as a wall hanging or decorative feature.

**YARN.** Medium-weight macramé twine, or any strong linen cord.

**MEASUREMENT.** Panel measures 18 in.

wide, 10 in. long to midway point of central pattern section (excluding fringe).

**PREPARATION.** Cut 96 threads, each 8 ft. long. Double them and set them with reversed double half hitches on to a double holding cord approximately 2 ft. long (192 working ends).

**TENSION CHECK.** One motif of first pattern section measures 1 in. long by $\frac{3}{4}$ in. wide.

**TO MAKE.** Attach double leader cords, approximately 2 ft. long, at left-hand side of work, and work a row of horizontal cording right across. Pin end of leader out of way of knotting, as it will be no longer required.

**Pattern section 1.** Divide cords into groups of 8.

**To work one motif:** using cord 1 as leader, work a row of diagonal cording slanting down to the right with cords 2, 3 and 4.

Using cord 8 as leader, work diagonal cording slanting down to the left with cords 7, 6 and 5. Now link the leaders by knotting cord 1 over cord 8 and let cord 8 continue across work maintaining same downward slope, and knot cords 4, 3 and 2

over it. Cord 1 again becomes a leader and is used to continue diagonal cording slanting to the right with cords 5, 6 and 7. Now work central knot of motif: tie a half hitch with cord 6 round cords 4 and 5, then tie a half hitch with cord 3 also round cords 4 and 5.

With cord 8 still as leader bring it round a pin and work diagonal cording slanting to the right with cords 2, 3 and 4. Similarly bring cord 1 round a pin and work diagonal cording slanting to the left with cords 7, 6 and 5.

Link the leaders by knotting cord 8 over cord 1, and let cord 1 continue across work, maintaining same downward slope. Knot cords 4, 3 and 2 over it.

Similarly, let cord 8 continue across other side of work to form final downward diagonal and knot cords 5, 6 and 7 over it. Repeat this pattern motif across each group of 8 cords.

**Divider row 1:** attach a separate double leader cord, approximately 2 ft. long, to left-hand side of knotting, and work a row of horizontal cording right across. Pin end of leader out of way of knotting, as it will be no longer required.

**Pattern section 2.** Divide cords into groups of 3, and work spirals of half hitches, knotting the 3rd cord of each group round the first 2.

**Divider row 2:** as divider row 1.

**Pattern section 3.** Divide cords into groups of 16.

**Work on first group of 16:** work 3 rows of diagonal cording slanting to the right, each row immediately below the previous one, on the first 8 cords, and using the cord on the far left as leader for each row.

Similarly work 3 rows of diagonal cording slanting to the left with the next 8 cords, using cord on far right as leader for each row.

Link the point of the 'V' by tying a flat knot bead with the 4 central cords (2 from each side). Work 4 flat knots before taking the sinnet up and over itself.

Now work 3 rows of diagonal cording slanting down to the left, on first group of 8 cords, using cord on far right as leader for each row.

Similarly work 3 rows of diagonal cording slanting down to the right with the second group of 8 cords, and using cord on far left as leader for each row.

**Work on second group of 16:** work chains of double alternate half hitches with each group of 4 cords to depth of motif worked with the first 16-cord group.

Repeat these two 16-cord motifs across row.

**Divider row 3:** as divider row 1.

**Pattern section 4.** Work across section in assorted chains of single alternate half hitches, double alternate half hitches and 3-cord spirals — in any order wished.

Work to a depth of 1 in.

**Divider row 4:** as divider row 1.

Now divide cords into 3 groups of 64 cords each.

**Work on first group of 64:** work a buttonhole bar (half hitches worked from the same side but eased to lie flat) with cord 1 over cords 2 and 3: work knot 12 times in all, and let the bar curve gently towards centre of work (see illustration).

Now take cord 17 as leader and work diagonal cording slanting to the left (to join up with buttonhole bar just worked). Knot over it: cords 16, 15, 14, 13, 12, 11, 10, 9, 8, 7, 6, 5, 4, 3, 2 and 1.

Take cord 18 as leader, and work a row of diagonal cording immediately below the previous one, and knotting with the same cords as before.

Now work 8 buttonhole knots with cord 17 over the 2 cords immediately to its right (cords 18 and 1).

Work another double row of diagonal cording in a similar way using cord 19 for first leader, cord 20 for second leader.

Work 6 buttonhole knots with cord 19 over cords 20 and 17.

Take cords 21 and 22 together as a double leader and work diagonal cording over them with all cords.

As you work, gradually ease knotting into the deep curved scallop, as shown in the illustration. The edge of the scallop is governed by the rows of buttonhole knots. The diagonal cording in every case is worked down to meet the end of the previous buttonhole bar.

Work 6 buttonhole knots with cord 21 over the 2 cords to its right (cords 22 and 19).

Now work another double row of diagonal cording, using cord 23 as first leader, cord 24 as second leader.

Work 6 buttonhole knots with cord 23 over cords 24 and 21. Work another double row of diagonal cording with cord 25 as first leader, cord 26 as second leader.

Work 6 buttonhole knots with cord 25 over cords 26 and 23.

Take cords 27 and 28 together as a double leader and work diagonal cording with all cords.

Work 4 buttonhole knots with cord 27 over cords 28 and 25. Work a double row of diagonal cording, using cord 29 as first leader, cord 30 as second leader. (**Note.** Rows of cording will appear almost vertical by this time, but you are still using the diagonal cording technique to work them.) Now work a banister bar with cords 31, 32, 33 and 34 to depth of last row of cording. Working from the right-hand side of scallop, repeat knotting sequence as worked for left-hand side, beginning with 12 buttonhole knots worked with cord 64 over cords 62 and 63. Cord 48 will then be the leader for first row of diagonal cording slanting to the right.

cord 1 of second-last motif continue as leader slanting to the right, knotting over it cords 2, 3 and 4 of the last motif. Work a third row in a similar way, with only 4 complete motifs plus a diagonal at each end. Then work a fourth row, with 2 complete motifs, plus a diagonal at each end. The final row will only have the 2 diagonals in it, in an inverted 'V'. Contain the pointed pattern section by working diagonal cording down each side. Use cord 8 from first motif as leader for cording down left-hand side; cord 1 from last motif as leader for cording down right-hand side.

Link the leaders at tip of point by knotting left-hand leader over right-hand leader. Work single alternate half hitch chains with each pair of cords to a depth of about 1 in.

Work another row of diagonal cording down each side, with cord on far left as leader for left-hand side; cord on far right as leader for right-hand side.

Work banister bars with each group of 4 cords to a depth of about 1 inch, and leave ends to form fringe.

**Work third group of 64 cords** to match first curved scallop.

**TO FINISH.** Trim tassels and centre fringe evenly to depth required. Fold ends of leader cords on to wrong side of work, laying them along the back of horizontal cording, and with needle and fine thread stitch them neatly in place.

Continue in this way working to match first half of scallop.

When the centre of scallop is reached, the cords from the left and right are crossed smoothly over each other behind the banister bar already worked, then all of them are drawn down to centre point of scallop.

Using the knotting cords from the banister bar, work a collecting knot tightly round all the cords to form a tassel.

**Work on second group of 64 cords:** this central pattern section is worked in criss-cross diagonal cording in groups of 8 cords. To work the first group, cord 1 is used as leader slanting to the right, and cords 2, 3 and 4 are knotted over it.

Then cord 8 is taken as leader slanting to the left and cords 7, 6 and 5 are knotted over it. The leaders are linked by knotting cord 1 over cord 8, then cord 8 continues slanting to the left and cords 4, 3 and 2 are knotted over it.

Cord 1 continues as leader slanting to the right and cords 5, 6 and 7 are knotted over it. Repeat this knotting sequence across row with each group of 8 cords.

**2nd row:** knot cord 1 of first motif over cord 8 of second motif, and continue with cord 8 of second motif as leader, slanting to the left, and knotting cords 7, 6 and 5 of first motif over it.

Work 8-cord motif across row 6 times. At end of row knot cord 8 of last motif over cord 1 of second-last motif and let

# *String doll*

Illustrated opposite

**YARN.** Medium-weight parcel string.

**YOU WILL ALSO NEED.** 7 wooden rods in the following sizes: 9 in., 6 in., 4½ in., and 2 each of 5 in. and 4 in. Wooden balls in the following sizes: one at 3 in. for head, 9 at 1 in. for neck, shoulders, hem ends, hands and feet, 10 at ½ in. for other points.

**MEASUREMENT.** Total length of doll 30 in.

**Note.** This design is really a method of displaying a sampler in an attractive and unusual way. Therefore the instructions here serve only as a guide: the precise knotting patterns used for each panel of the main

section can take any form you wish.

**ARMS AND LEGS. Preparation.** Cut 8 threads each 72 in. Double them and set them with reversed double half hitches on to the 9 in. wooden rod, arranging cords in two groups of 4 each at either end of the rod (8 working ends in each group). Insert a 1 in. wooden ball on to each end of the rod.

**To make.** Work on first group of 8 ends: Work 2 chains of Genoese bars (alternate half hitches over central core), with 4 cords in each chain: 2 outer knotting cords, 2 central knot-bearing core cords. When chains measure approximately 5 in., work a multi-end flat knot to link the chains. Take all cord ends through a 1 in. wooden ball. Cut 8 threads, each 5 in. long, and set them with reversed double half hitches on to a circular holding cord. Tie holding cord tightly round threads coming from the wooden balls, to form fingers.

Repeat with a second group of 8 ends to form other arm and fingers.

Work legs and feet in a similar way, setting threads on to a 6-in. wooden rod, working chains to 7 in., and cutting threads for feet to 6 in.

## MAIN BODY SECTION. Preparation.

Set number of cords required on to rod holding worked arms: the number you use will depend on the knotting pattern you wish to work. Our doll has 18 cords set on (36 working ends) each cut to 13 ft. 6 in.

**To make.** Each panel of pattern should be worked to depth required, then a cording divider row worked over a wooden rod. New cords can be added in the cording rows by setting on with double half hitches, if extra width is required.

Our doll is worked in the following pattern sequence:

**Panel 1:** 12-cord cording diamonds, linked with flat knots, and having a multi-end flat knot central motif in complete diamonds, overhand knots in the half motifs at each side.

Cording divider over 5-in. rod.

**Panel 2:** Genoese bars to depth of $2\frac{1}{2}$ in.

Cording divider over 4-in. rod.

**Panel 3:** alternate flat knot pattern (3 rows).

Cording divider over 4-in. rod.

**Panel 4:** as panel 2.

Cording divider over $4\frac{1}{2}$ in. rod.

**Panel 5:** 12-cord narrow leaf motifs linked in centre with flat knots.

Cording divider over 5-in. rod.

**Panel 6:** flat knots in a spasmodic arrangement.

Cording divider (no rod).

**Panel 7:** cording diamonds (12 cords to 2 central motifs, 6 to half motifs at sides). Flat knots to link and as central motifs. Cording divider over 6 in. rod which already holds worked legs.

Tie overhand knots in each cord and trim ends to represent a skirt.

**HEAD.** Set on threads to circular holding cord sufficient to give length and quantity

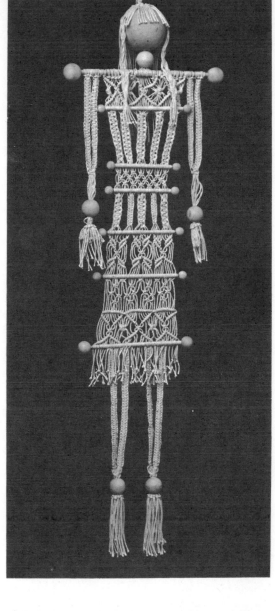

of hair required. Tighten holding cord and take ends through a 3-in. wooden ball (head) then down through a 1 in. wooden ball (neck) and attach to centre of shoulder wooden rod with double half hitches. Adjust hair on top of head, trim front to represent a fringe, arrange the remainder in 2 plaits. Tie ends of plaits with fine thread, and glue plaits lightly in place to side of head.

**TO FINISH.** Attach wooden balls to ends of remaining rods.

# White bikini

Illustrated in colour on page 126
**YARN.** We used Wendy Tricel Nylon 4-ply Crêpe, but any 4-ply knitting yarn should do. Preferably it should be one which washes well, is shrink resistant, and will not stretch.
**MEASUREMENT.** Bikini will fit an average bust size 34 in. The pattern can however be adapted to suit a bigger or smaller size by adding to or subtracting from outside edges. As the knotting pattern is a free one, individual fitting idiosyncrasies can be allowed for as you work. Knotting must be done over some sort of pattern guide — either the pattern given here, or to be sure of making a garment which will fit your shape and size, use as your guide an old well-fitting bikini, or else a bra and pants.
**TENSION CHECK.** This is difficult to give precisely as the pattern is free, and is based on working to a shape rather than a specific number of knots, but as an approximate

*Close-up showing detail of knotting on pants.*

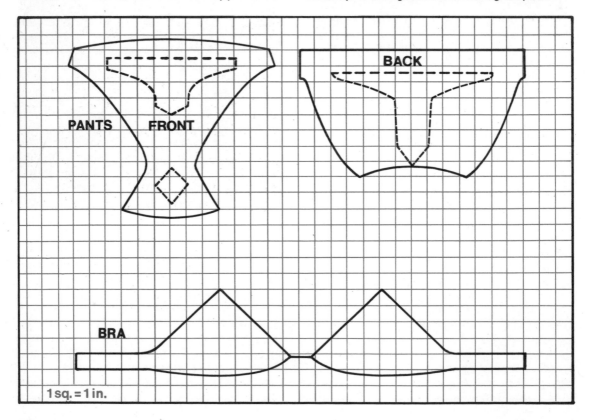

guide, in the yarn we used a single chain of 12 alternate half hitches (6 from each side) measures 1 in.

**PREPARATION.** The diagrams opposite show pattern pieces drawn to scale (1 square represents 1 inch). Following these diagrams as a guide, work out your full-size pattern on tissue, squared or brown paper. Cut out the shapes — 2 pieces for the pants, 1 for the bra. Before main knotting begins, a Genoese bar is worked with 3 cords (2 outer knotting cords work half hitches alternately from each side over 1 central knot-bearing core cord) and pinned along lower edge of bra, and right round side and leg edges of pants. This gives a firm edging and as knotting proceeds working cords are looped into the braid.

For the pants you will need 2 braids, each about 2 ft. long: for each braid cut 2 knotting cords of approx. 8 ft., 1 central knot-bearing cord of about 3 ft. For the lower edge of bra you will need a braid about 28 in. long: cut 2 knotting cords of 10 ft., 1 knot-bearing cord of 3 ft. Setting on and lengths of working cords are given in the course of making instructions which follow.

**TO MAKE PANTS. Front.** First make 2 Genoese bar braids each 2 ft. long (see Preparation above). Now pin pattern piece for pants front to working surface, pinning it so gusset edge is at top, waist edge at bottom. Beginning at lower left-hand corner of shape (waist edge) pin one braid from this point right round side and leg edges of pants. This way pin other braid to right-hand edge (the remainder of each braid will be used to continue edging round sides of pants back — pin the excess braid meanwhile to working surface out of the way of knotting).

Now lay a holding cord across curved top edge of gusset. Pin in place and set on 10 threads, each 6 ft. 6 in. long, to the centre of the holding cord, doubling them and setting them on with reversed double half hitches (20 working ends).

Using cord on far left as leader, work 2 rows of horizontal cording.

Now set on a new thread at each end of knotting to gusset holding cord, each thread cut to 6 ft. 6 in. (24 working ends).

Continue to work in rows of horizontal cording but spacing rows slightly so they do not give solid cording but rather an open-work, lacy effect (the spacing can be as much or as little as you wish).

Leaders can be taken from left or right-hand side of work.

Continue to set on extra threads (all 6 ft. 6 in.) to each end of work until you reach the side edge braids. Continue working in rows of horizontal cording, but at the end of each row carefully loop the leader cord through the braid.

After about 8 rows of cording, divide cords into 2 equal groups, and work 10 rows of cording on each group, using outer cords as leader for every row and leaving each leader hanging in centre as row is completed. (i.e. do not knot it on to leader of subsequent row).

Now fill in the whole of this central area (indicated by dotted lines on pattern diagram) with the alternate flat knot pattern. When the flat knot diamond is complete continue working fairly free rows of cording, first on either side of the lower section of flat-knot diamond, and then right across work. Loop new threads on to the side-edge braids where necessary to increase width of work. As work proceeds, new threads can of course be cut considerably shorter than the early ones.

Fill in another area of flat knots, where indicated by dotted lines on the pattern diagram.

Finish at waist edge with 8 rows of solid horizontal cording (to give firm edge).

**Back.** Unpin pants front, turn it round, so waist edge is at top, and re-pin to working surface. Pin pattern for pants back to working surface below worked pants front, so gusset edges fit together. Pin braids from side edges of front round shaped edges of back as far as lower corners (waist edge).

Set on 18 threads each 5 ft. to centre of holding cord of front (along gusset edge). Now work in a similar way as for front, in free rows of horizontal cording, adding new threads as necessary at side edges, looping into the braid, and working a 'T' shape of flat knots in the centre, as indicated by dotted lines on pattern diagram. Finish waist edge with 8 rows of solid horizontal cording.

**TO FINISH PANTS.** Using a crochet hook bring each cord through from back to front of work between the 2nd last and 3rd last rows of cording. Tie each group of 4 cords in a flat knot, then working in alternate sequence from flat knots, tie each group of 4 cords in an overhand knot. Trim ends to form tassels of about 4 in. Finish ends of side braids in the same way.

**To make ties.** Cut 5 cords each 10 ft., double them and set them on by reversed double half hitches to braid at left side edge of pants front. Tie each pair of set-on cords in a single alternate half hitch chain for 2 in. Then tie a multi-end flat knot to link all cords together. Trim away 4 cords after the multi-end flat knot, and continuing on 6 cords, tie a multi-end flat knot chain, spacing knots at approx. 1 in. intervals.

When chain measures approx. 14 in. divide cords into 3 groups of 2 cords each, and finish with 3 chains of single alternate half hitches worked to about 3 in. Make tie for right front side edge in a similar way, also for both side edges of pants back.

**TO MAKE THE BRA.** Make a Genoese bar braid on 3 cords, as for pants, to measure approx. 28 in. This will form lower edge of bra. Now cut 3 cords, each 8 yd.

Set them on to a very short holding cord, and using cord on far left as leader, work a zig-zag cording braid for about 18 in.

Divide cords into 2 groups of 3, and work a Genoese bar braid with each group, the right-hand braid to 6 in., the left-hand braid to 12 in.

Make another similar cording and Genoese bar braid but this time after dividing cords make right-hand braid 12 in., left-hand one 6 in.

**Work on right-hand side of bra only.** Pin pattern piece to working surface and beginning at lower left-hand corner pin lower edge braid in place. Pin the first cording and Genoese bar braid to other edges of pattern so point where braids divide is at top of triangle.

Cut 4 threads, each 6 ft. Double them and set them with reversed double half hitches on to last row of cording on cording braid. Tie a flat knot with each group of 4 cords.

Add a new thread at each side, looping it into braid as before, and tie 3 flat knots in the alternate sequence.

Continue to work in the alternate flat knot pattern of 2-knot sinnets of flat knots. When at each side on every row until the full width of triangle is reached. Now cut 30 threads each 18 in., double them and set them with reversed double half hitches on to lower cord of remaining braid edging (which will form back of bra).

Continue to work across all cords in alternate pattern of 2-knot sinnets of flat knots. When lower braid edging is reached carefully thread each cord through first and 3rd cords of the braid on the wrong side of work (take care not to catch in the centre knot-bearing cord of braid). Ends of braid from top edges similarly should be threaded through lower edge braid.

In a similar way work left-hand side of bra, leaving about an inch of lower edge braid between the 2 knotted sections.

**TO FINISH BRA.** To shape the bra, carefully pull central knot-bearing core cords of lower edge braid at each side. Provided this cord has not been caught into the knotting at any point this should gather up the lower edge to give curved cup shapes for each side of bra. When shaping is sufficient, tie an overhand knot at each end of braid close to finished knotting and trim away ends. Finish these side edges with ties as for pants, but only set on 3 double cords (not 5) and do not trim away any ends after the first alternate half hitch chains have been worked.

Along the lower edge tie each group of 4 cords in a flat knot, then finish below the flat knot with an overhand knot. Trim ends to leave tassels of approx. 2½ in.

Turn the end of each shoulder strap (cording braid) back on itself for about 2 in., and stitch to form a loop — the ties from back of bra will slot through these loops and be used to fasten bra.

## Fringed waistcoat

Illustrated on page 168.
**YARN.** Dishcloth cotton in white.

**YOU WILL ALSO NEED.** 2 linked decorative buttons.

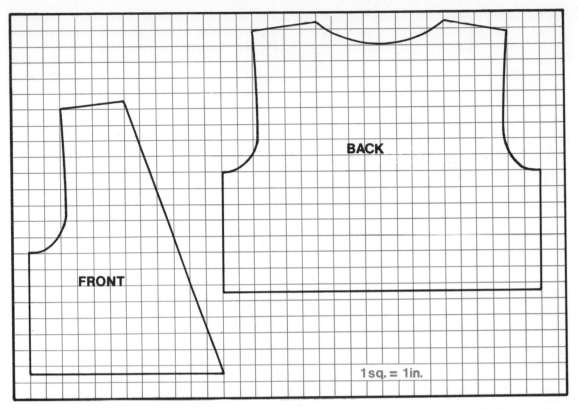

FRONT

BACK

1 sq. = 1in.

**MEASUREMENT.** Finished waistcoat should fit an average bust size 34/36 in. Back length (excluding fringe) 15½ in.

**TENSION CHECK.** 4 flat knots measure 1 in.

**PREPARATION.** In order to achieve shaping for waistcoat (e.g. round armhole curves, shoulder line etc.) it is best to work over a paper pattern. The diagrams above show the pattern shape drawn to scale (1 square represents 1 inch). Following these diagrams as a guide, work out your full-size pattern on tissue, squared or brown paper. Cut out the shapes (1 for the waistcoat back, 1 for the waistcoat front).

For each waistcoat front, cut 16 threads at 10 ft., 2 at 6 ft., 2 at 5 ft. 6 in., 8 at 5 ft., 1 at 7 ft., and 1 at 5 yd.

For back waistcoat, cut 32 threads at 10 ft., 4 at 6 ft., 4 at 5 ft. 6 in., 16 at 5 ft., 2 at 7 ft., 32 at 9 ft. 6 in., and 1 at 3 ft. Cut 4 holding cords (for shoulder edges) each 1 ft.

Setting on for back and front will be described in the course of making instructions which follow.

**TO MAKE.** Work on right front of waistcoat first.

Pin paper pattern piece to working surface then pin one holding cord along shoulder edge. Set 16 threads at 10 ft. on to this, doubling them and setting them on with reversed double half hitches but have the knot of the reversed double half hitch on the wrong side of work (32 working ends). At armhole edge set on one 7 ft. thread; and at centre front edge set on the 5 yd. thread, but set on this thread so the inside working cord measures approx. 2 ft., and all the extra length is on the outside cord (at centre front edge).

Pin centre front cords (both of them) in place following outline of pattern. Similarly at armhole edge pin the 2 cords round curved shaping of armhole.

Now begin knotting pattern:

**1st row:** leave first 2 cords (armhole edge) unworked; work sinnets of 4 flat knots with each group of 4 cords: 8 sinnets altogether; leave last 2 cords (centre front edge) unworked.

**Next row:** tie single flat knots with each group of 4 cords, so the first knot will be tied with the 2 armhole edge cords and cords 1 and 2 from first 4-knot sinnet; last

knot will be tied with cords 3 and 4 of the last sinnet together with the 2 cords at centre front edge. (You will of course have to unpin outer cords in order to tie knots, but as soon as row is worked, re-pin armhole and centre front cords to pattern shape).

Continue in this pattern until 5 rows of 4-knot sinnets have been worked altogether. Now carefully set on to the 2 armhole edge cords (treating them as a double thickness holding cord) the two 6 ft. threads (set them on so they are approx. in line with the midway point of the 4-knot sinnets just worked). Work sinnets of 2 flat knots with these 4 new cords.

**Next row:** in a similar way set on a 5 ft. 6 in. thread to armhole edge cords. Work single flat knots across row, tying first knot with the 2 new cords and cords 1 and 2 of the 2-knot sinnet of previous row.

**Next row:** set on another 5 ft. 6 in. thread, and work 4-knot sinnets across row (first sinnet will be tied with the new cords and the new cords set on in previous row). Making sure double cords at armhole edge are pinned exactly to pattern shape, set on remaining 8 threads of 5 ft. each. Working on these new cords (from left to right), work 3 sinnets of 2 flat knots each, 1 sinnet of 3 flat knots.

All cords across work should now line up. Work a row of single flat knots all the way across. Then continue in pattern until another 4 bands of pattern have been worked, ending with the single knot row.

(**Note.** In order to maintain slope of centre front edge, sinnets will gradually have to be spaced out towards lower edge. Take care to keep side edge perfectly straight.)

Now carefully unpin work, and unpinning pattern piece reverse it so it will form left front of waistcoat. Pin it to working surface, and proceed with knotting for left front to match right front.

When knotting is complete, unpin left front carefully. Now pin pattern piece for back waistcoat to working surface. Pin remaining 2 holding cords of 1 ft. to each shoulder edge. Set on 16 threads of 10 ft. to each holding cord.

Set on a 7 ft. thread to form each armhole edge. Set on the 3 ft. thread to form back neckline, setting it on one shoulder holding cord, pinning it carefully round curve of neckline and attaching ends to other shoulder holding cord with double half hitches.

Set on remaining 32 threads of 9 ft. 6 in. round this neckline edge, spacing them evenly.

Now begin knotting pattern as for front, adding new cords at armhole edges exactly as for front. The first pair of cords on neckline at each side will be brought into the knotting pattern on the first row of single knots, the remainder on the following 4-knot sinnets.

Continue in pattern until back measures the same as front. Carefully unpin work.

**TO FINISH.** Sew fronts to back along shoulder edges with neat overhand stitches (if preferred, these seams can be avoided by setting threads for back directly on to set-on (shoulder) edges of front).

Now link front to back at the sides by tying a flat knot with the 2 pairs of armhole edge cords (one from front, one from back). Continue to tie a chain of flat knots with these cords, lacing them through loops of side edges of back and front to draw edges together.

Now beginning at lower centre front point of right front, take long holding cord and using it as a leader work cording along lower edge of right front and the back as far as centre back. Similarly work cording along lower edge of left front and back to centre back using holding cord from left front centre edge as leader. Link the two leaders by knotting one over the other. Trim fringe evenly all round to depth required. Fasten waistcoat at centre front points with linked buttons, using holes in knotting pattern as buttonholes.

*Fringed waistcoat in white cotton yarn (see page 166).*

# Glossary of terms

**Banister bar** – a spiral of half knots worked continuously from the same side.

**Bar** – a chain of knots which has a knot-bearing core.

**Bead knot** – a 'solid' knot formed on the surface of work by a short chain of flat knots taken up and over itself.

**Berry knot** – an interesting textural knot formed from a closely worked motif of cording.

**Buttonhole bar** – chain of half hitches worked continuously from the same side over one or more knot-bearing cords, with the knots eased to lie flat.

**Carrick bend** – another name for the Josephine knot.

**Cavandoli work** – a two-colour technique based on closely-worked horizontal and vertical cording. Background colour is worked in horizontal cording, the design picked out in vertical cording in the contrast colour.

**Chain** – usually refers to the chain formed by half hitches worked alternately from the left and right.

**Chinese crown knot** – a fancy knot similar in appearance to the true lover's knot, but worked in a different way.

**Clove hitch** – another name for the double half hitch.

**Coil knot** – a knot used to finish ends.

**Collecting knot** – any knot used to collect groups of cords together.

**Cording** – a line of double half hitches worked closely together in a horizontal, vertical or diagonal direction.

**Core** – the central knot-bearing cords of a knot.

**Corkscrew bar** – half hitches worked continuously from one side round one or more knot-bearing cords.

**Cow hitch** – another name for the reversed double half hitch.

**Double half hitch** – the half hitch knot worked twice.

**Flat knot** – one of the two basic knots, formed by tying two half knots, one from the left, one from the right.

**Genoese bar** – a chain of half hitches worked alternately from the left and right over a central knot-bearing core.

**Half hitch** – one of the two basic knots formed by looping one cord around another.

**Half knot** – the first part of a flat knot.

**Holding cord** – length of yarn on which working threads are mounted.

**Japanese knot** – a fancy knot formed from an ornamental arrangement of flat knots.

**Josephine knot** – one of the fancy knots, formed from two knotting ends closely laced with each other.

**Knot-bearing cord** – the cord on which a knot is tied, and which should be kept taut.

**Knotting cord** – the cord which is used to tie a knot.

**Lark's head** – another name for the reversed double half hitch.

**Leader cord** – the foundation or knot-bearing cord on which cording is worked. The direction and angle of finished cording depends on the direction and angle in which the leader is held.

**Macramé knot** – another name for the flat knot.

**Marling knot** – an overhand knot tied in one cord over another placed at right angles to it.

**Monkey's fist** – a solid, three-dimensional knot usually worked over a bead, marble or other hard surface.

**Overhand knot** — knot used to anchor holding cord to working surface, and frequently to finish off work. Can also be used in a knotting pattern.

**Reversed double half hitch** — the knot used to mount threads; it can also be used in a knotting pattern, and is formed by working a half hitch followed by a half hitch in the reverse direction.

**Sailor's knot** — another name for the flat knot.

**Setting on threads** — mounting working threads on to a holding cord, a rod, a ring, or the edge of fabric.

**Shell knot** — another form of the bead knot.

**Simple knot** — another name for the half hitch.

**Sinnet** — a single chain of knots worked continuously.

**Solomon's bar** — a chain of flat knots.

**Solomon's knot** — another name for the flat knot.

**Square knot** — another name for the flat knot.

**Tatted bar** — a chain of reversed double half hitches.

**Triple knot** — a flat knot followed by a half knot.

**True lover's knot** — two linked overhand knots.

**Turk's head** — a solid, three-dimensional knot.

**Waved bar** — chain formed by knotting groups of five or seven half hitches alternately from the right and left over a central knot-bearing core.

# Books to read

The following list represents a selection of books published since the 19th century which contain valuable references to macramé work and knotting techniques. The recently published titles should be readily available through most booksellers. The older books however may not be so easy to obtain, but are well worth trying to track down — a determined search in second-hand and junk shops should prove profitable. Alternatively, the books can usually be consulted at most good reference libraries.

**Anchor Manual of Needlework**
Batsford Ltd., London 3rd edition 1968

**The Ashley Book of Knots**
**Clifford Ashley**
Doubleday & Co., New York 1944

**Macramé, The Art of Creative Knotting**
Virginia I. Harvey
Van Nostrand Reinhold Co., New York 1967

**Macramé, Creative Design in Knotting**
Dona Z. Meilach
Crown Publishers Inc., New York 1971

**Macramé, Creative Knotting**
Imelda Manalo Pesch
Sterling Publishing Co. Inc., New York 1970

**Le Macramé**
Thérèse de Dillmont
DMC Library, Mulhouse, France c. 1880

**Designing with String**
Mary Seyd
Batsford, London 1963

**Step-by-step Macramé**
Mary Walker Phillips
Golden Press, New York 1970

**Introducing Macramé**
Eirian Short
Batsford, London 1970

**Encyclopedia of Needlework**
Thérèse de Dillmont
DMC Library, Mulhouse, France c. 1880
(this book has recently been re-published in facsimile)

**The History of Needlework Tools and Accessories**
Sylvia Groves
The Hamlyn Publishing Group, England 1966

**Tying Knots**
Eric Franklin
C. Arthur Pearson Ltd., London 2nd ed. 1966

**Encyclopedia of Knots and Fancy Rope Work**
Raoul M. Graumont and John Hensel
Cornell Maritime Press 4th ed. 1970

**A History of Lace**
Mrs. Bury Palliser
Sampson, Low, Marston and Co., London 1902

**Dictionary of Needlework**
S. F. A. Caulfeild and B. C. Saward
L. Upcott Gill, London 1903

**Weldon's Practical Needlework**
Weldon's Ltd., London c. 1900

**Point and Pillow Lace**
A. M. Sharp 1899

**Sylvia's Book of Macramé Lace**
Ward Lock, London 1882

**Macramé Lace Book**
London, 1874

**Lindhorst-Macramé,** Volumes 1 and 2
P. Lindhorst, London c. 1900

**Every Woman's Encyclopaedia**
23 Bouverie St., London c. 1910

# Acknowledgements

To very many people I owe grateful thanks for help with my search for examples of modern and historical macramé work, and information about the craft. Of the many who gave freely of their time to offer help, advice and suggestions, I am indebted to: Miss Levey, of the Victoria and Albert Museum, London; Miss R. P. Prentice, of the National Maritime Museum; Miss A. Buck, of the Gallery of English Costume, Manchester; Mrs. V. Cliffe and Mrs. J. A. B. Barker, of the Bath College of Education; Mrs. S. Tan, of the Hornsey School of Art; Mrs. C. Parker, of University of London Goldsmiths' College; Miss Alexandra Beale, of the Embroiderers' Guild; Mrs. Eirian Short, of Camberwell, London; Mrs. N. Kimmins, of Beckenham, Kent; Mrs. J. Fogg, of Bromley, Kent; Mrs. Wall of Eastbourne, Sussex; Mr. Bo Ridley, of London; Mr. B. P. C. Bridgewater, of the British Museum.

To Mrs. M. Craske, of Bromley, Kent, who bravely accepted my challenge to design and make up a knotted bikini for the pattern chapter, I say a particular thank you. Finally, my grateful thanks to my step-daughter Caroline who gave up most of her school summer holiday in order to help me make the samplers and examples of knotting patterns. Acknowledgements are also due to the following people and organisations who generously loaned work or photographs from their collection, or made up designs.

**Embroiderers' Guild:** table runner, page 15; Cavandoli bag, page 17; Chinese banner, page 28; Moroccan panel, page 35; Chinese overskirt, page 35; glove puppet on page 108 (made by Ingrid Rowling).

**Victoria and Albert Museum:** historic examples shown on pages 12 (Italian bands), 18, 25, 40, 47, 79, 95, 118.

**National Maritime Museum:** sailor's wall pockets, page 10.

**City of Manchester Art Galleries:** gloves, page 12; bags on page 39.

**British Museum:** quipu, page 7.

**Bo Ridley:** fashion garments and jewellery pages 36, 54 (room divider), 58, 67, 71, 127, 132; also shawl on front cover.

**Mrs. J. Fogg:** bags on pages 80, 129 and back cover.

**Mrs. V. Dean:** Victorian baby's bonnet, page 14; Victorian wall panel, page 160.

**Mrs. M. Craske:** lampshade, page 103; string doll page 163; white bikini, page 164.

**Miss E. Love:** belts on pages 43, 87, 119 and 133.

**Mrs. Eirian Short:** hanging on pages 54 and 81; multicolour belt on page 144.

**K. H. Bailey:** beaded choker, page 145.

**R. Mathias:** hipster string belt, page 142.

**Caroline Bailey:** three-colour belt, page 144; square motif bag, page 154.

**Shelley Churchman:** hanging on pages 5 and 66; sampler on page 59.

**Alex Ward:** knotted sculptures on pages 19 and 125.

**Carole Semaine,** Hornsey School of Art: three-colour shawl, page 89.

**Susan Coward,** Hornsey School of Art: two rug wool samplers, page 40.

**Joanna Bowring,** Hornsey School of Art: notebooks on pages 27 and 113.

**Norma Day,** Hornsey School of Art: white Cavandoli sampler, page 93.

**Kim Chenoweth,** Hornsey School of Art: necklaces and cravat, pages 127 and 128; heavy wool rug, page 89; piping cord rug, page 112; nine sampler pictures, page 137.

**Marion Hicks,** 2nd year diploma student in art and design, Goldsmiths' College: sculptured head, page 53 and on back cover; chess set, page 72; hanging and belts on page 90; light pull, page 134.

**Mrs. Suni Wysman,** Goldsmiths' College: reverse cording belts, page 133.

**Mrs. J. A. B. Barker,** Bath College of Education: sampler belt, page 136.

**Pauline Oddy,** Bath College of Education: Fiesta hanging on back cover.

**Maggi Tucker,** Bath College of Education: string bag, page 38.

**Beth Anslow,** Bath College of Education: rug wool bag, page 72.

**Jackie Garrett,** Bath College of Education: bead sampler, page 128.

**Hobby Horse Ltd.,** 15–17 Langton St., London S.W.10 (from whom yarns, instruction leaflets and beads may be ordered): envelope bag and beaded bag, page 149.

**The Needlewoman Shop,** Regent St., London W.1, who loaned yarns and materials.

**John and Mary Chaloner Woods** – who took most of the photographs.

# Index